PREPARING
your
DAUGHTER
for
WOMANHOOD

A GUIDE FOR MOMS

Robin Jones Gunn

For my granddaughter(s)
and their daughters and granddaughters

Contents

1. Hello, Beautiful Reader 13

2. Heart to Heart 21

3. Learn Her Language 35

4. Make Your Plan 49

5. Normalize Respect 67

6. Celebrate the Moment 85

7. Make Peace with Your Past....................... 99

8. Focus on the Future................................ 117

9. Bring the Sacred.................................... 133

10. Women Like Us.................................... 151

My Hope for You..................................... 169

More Than: A Poem for My Daughter......... 172

What God Says about You 177

A Daughter's Wish

Come to me when my heart is young
I want you, Mom, to be the one
Who reveals the mysteries
Of what is to come
When my heart is still young.

Hello, Beautiful Reader

*Gracious words are a
honeycomb,
sweet to the soul
and healing to the bones.*

Proverbs 16:24, NIV

Chapter One

Hello, Beautiful Reader

All the signs are there, aren't they? Your daughter is changing. Each day seems to propel her closer to puberty—how did she grow up so quickly?

You want this change to be a positive experience for her. You want her to feel good about herself and her body. But how can you do that? How can you enter in when all she wants to do is be alone in her room?

I see you. I know what you're feeling. I applaud you for being intentional about this.

This book will help you to create significant, positive moments with your daughter. You'll find ideas on how to connect with her in a way that will profoundly deepen your relationship and bond the two of you together in the years ahead.

This is your chance to make a sacred fuss over her.

Don't pull back. It doesn't matter how you ended up in the role of "mom" in her life, whether by birth or another happy blessing. The undeniable fact is that you are the most important voice in her coming-of-age story. Even if your input seems unwanted right now, what she will remember years from now is that you cared enough to make this milestone comfortable and affirming for her.

You can do this. You really can.

Why I Care

When my daughter was maturing, I asked friends for ideas on how they marked their daughters' journeys into womanhood. A few of them shared personal stories about their own experiences and how things rolled out with their daughters, but only a few had suggestions on how to enter this season in a positive way.

I was determined to celebrate the change. So, knowing how much my little girl loved tea parties, music, and dance, I planned a Welcome to Womanhood party for Rachel. Simple, sweet, cozy, and intimate. Just what she liked. The party was a success, and soon other moms asked what I did. I was invited to keynote on the subject at women's events and on radio programs. I even wrote a gift book entitled *Gentle Passages: Guiding Your Daughter into Womanhood*.

When that book went out of print, the requests kept coming from moms of preteen girls for an updated book that gave more direction and advice. Many of the young moms who wrote to me had grown up reading my Christy Miller novels and were looking for mentoring advice now that their daughters were entering their teen years.

I knew I needed to write a new book—this book. So I brought up the topic on social media. The flood of responses surprised me. I heard from women all over the world. Some of the stories brought me to tears because of the pain of those women's journeys into adolescence. Others made me smile at the creativity. I've drawn from and combined excerpts of those comments in the "Moms and Daughters" section at the end of each chapter.

I also discovered something interesting about you, dear mothers everywhere. I learned that as you watch your daughter grow into the springtime of her life, you're well aware that you are moving farther along into the summer of your days. Certain patterns have been established. Certain relationships haven't changed. Old hurts bubble to the surface. Complicated feelings rise in you alongside the elevated hormone changes in your daughter.

Why do some things about her suddenly bother you so much? How did the interactions between your daughter and you become so messy? What happened to the sweet and silly girl who used to make you laugh? Why is she glaring at you, and why do you want to say things to her that you never imagined would come out of your mouth?

Both of you are changing. At the same time.

Physically, emotionally, mentally, spiritually, it's a tsunami of change. Premenopausal meets preadolescence is no joke.

That's why I've included some chapters in this book specifically for you and focused on what you need as you head into this next season as a woman and a mother. I knew that it wouldn't be enough to write a book that simply tossed creative projects at you so that you would have lots of ideas for a new Pinterest page. I wanted to help you to prepare for the next season in ways that are life-giving for you as well as for your daughter. When you are at your best, when your heart is at peace and filled up, you will have an abundance of everything you need to give to your daughter.

Start the Conversation

Giving out of abundance is much different from going through the motions of having "the talk" so you could say you did what was expected of you.

You are not having "the talk." You are starting the conversation.

That's the objective here. You are initiating one of many valuable conversations. You're building a bridge that the two of you can use many times in the years ahead to easily journey back and forth into each other's lives. Gaining access to her heart and opening yours to her starts now.

I hope you noticed that *Preparing Your Daughter for Womanhood* isn't designed to be handed to a young girl. It's for you—the mom, the dad, the mentor, the sister, or the grandmother—to equip you to be proactive in a young girl's life and to instill in her coming-of-age transition a sense of the sacred as well as of celebration of her.

Have you also noticed that it's not possible to separate a daughter from her mother? No matter what the relationship is like, no matter how many issues or miles or other people come between the two of you in the years ahead, an invisible thread will always connect you.

My daughter is now married with children of her own,

and our close relationship is one of my most treasured gifts. We've both had to work on our communication, and we've had plenty of do-overs. Grace upon grace has brought us to where we are today, and I'm so grateful. I asked for her input on this book, and what she added was golden. She brought touches of beauty, just as she does in all areas of her life.

She and I both look back and see that the Welcome to Womanhood Party I put together for her when she was nine established a structure and pattern for our relationship that was far more valuable than either of us realized at the time. That was the day we laid the foundation for the friendship we both cherish today. I wish you the same bridge-building experience.

All Moms Are Included

I want you to know that even if your childhood was bumpy, this book will help to equip you. If your relationship with your daughter isn't all you had dreamed it would be, this book can help to change the trajectory. If you already have a good relationship with your daughter, you can still improve it by making this transition time in her life a lovely and honoring experience for her.

Preparing Your Daughter for Womanhood will undoubtedly find its way into the hands of many moms, stepmoms, grandmas, aunts, sisters, mentors, counselors, and even some dads. Please know that I am including all of you in the term "mom" that appears on these pages. Think of the "daughter" throughout the book as that young girl who has been entrusted to you. Your role as the mother figure in her life, regardless of how you came into that position, allows you to become one of the clearest, truest, most loving voices that will speak into her life. She needs to be able to trust you rather than look elsewhere for the messages she longs to hear.

Other sources will give input into her life and provide details of how her body will soon change. Some already have. Other voices—online, through books, classrooms, and even sleepovers—will provide information. But will any of them speak the powerful words of affirmation she needs? Will any of them add the celebration? Will they elevate and honor her? That privilege lies with you.

You are the one who can bring a sense of the sacred into this natural passage from childhood to womanhood.

I'm excited to tell you how.

Heart to Heart

But you, O Lord, know me;
You see me and test me—my heart is with you.

Jeremiah 12:3a, NRSV

Chapter Two

Heart to Heart

Do you believe every young girl needs to know that she is intricately and wonderfully created by God? Do you agree that being female is a beautiful, complicated mystery and that your daughter is a one-of-a-kind woman with a future brimming with possibilities?

Good.

Then you and I have the same heart-to-heart belief. That's important because this book focuses on how you can communicate those foundational truths to your daughter. Your voice, your smiles, your clear eyes should always feel like home to her. You want her to believe that you see her and desire to know her.

You Are Her Haven

It's amazing to think of being her haven, isn't it? You are a destination. For the rest of her life, she can come to you. You want her to know that you are the safest person and a consistently open go-to destination in her life. You can create a relationship between the two of you in which she can always be herself, feel accepted, and settle in at any time for meaningful conversations.

The way she views her body, her personality, her appearance, and her abilities as well as her weaknesses will radically affect her for the rest of her life. She is most vulnerable during the stretch between childhood and adulthood. Her tender heart is the most open to both truth and lies.

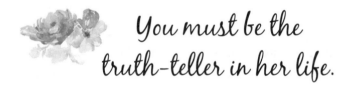

You must be the truth-teller in her life.

Your words hold great power, even if she seems to roll her eyes at everything you say. The truths and affirmations you're speaking will settle in her heart and stay with her throughout her life. Negative and derogatory comments—even ones she overhears—can grow deep roots during adolescence, which is why you must choose your words wisely.

She's listening and learning from the way you talk about your body, your relationships, and your feelings. What are the messages you've been sending her way?

God Is Your Haven

No matter how inadequate you feel about your crucial role with her, your daughter has been entrusted to you. God created her and brought her into your life. Believe that. Be thankful. God knew what He was doing when He gave her to you, in whatever way that happened—through birth, marriage, adoption, or a mentoring relationship. She came into your life, and you are now the one who can become her most influential and important mentor, influencer, and friend as the years go on.

Have you ever actually accepted that position in her life?

> *Here am I, and the children the LORD has given me.*
> Isaiah 8:18a, NIV

I remember the first time I came across this verse, and how it seemed to echo inside me. I paused and prayed the words as an act of resolution. I was saying, "God, I have no idea what I'm doing as a mother, but here I am, humbled and open-hearted to You. These are the children, the son and daughter, You've given me. I receive them as a gift from You."

That act of accepting the role I was already in as a mother allowed me to relinquish whatever control I thought I had and to step into a place of confidence, believing that God was in control. God gave these children to my husband and me. He loved them and cared about their lives far more than we ever could.

Do you believe that? It's a good place to start—or in some cases, to hit restart. Remind yourself that God is your haven. You can run to Him at any time. He sees your heart. He knows all your strengths as well as your inadequacies. You have never been alone in your role as a mom, and you're not alone now.

Mama Trauma

I hope you had, and still have, an affirming and nurturing relationship with your mother. If you did, some of the suggestions in this book will seem second nature to you.

However, not all of us grew up with a strong connection to our moms. Many of us look back and see that we were not nurtured or instructed in a way that instilled confidence or freedom. Instead, we matured under the shadow of a sense of insecurity and shame.

If that's where you're coming from, you're not alone. Most women who shared details about their growing-up years with me said that when they were ushered into puberty, the experience was a negative one. As a result, they are at a loss now on how to do it differently for their daughter. This is what they told me:

- I don't know what to say.

- She already knows the basics. Isn't that enough?

- I don't want to embarrass her.

- I'm nervous that she'll ask questions I won't want to answer or know how to answer.

- I think she already knows she can come to me if she has any questions.

- She's still so young. I don't want to spoil any of her innocence.

Can you relate to any of those comments? I get it. Mama trauma is real.

Take a deep breath. Say a little prayer. Let your mindset shift toward the possibility of fresh beginnings.

The Why

Right now, it probably seems like being her mama when she was little was easier. She relied on you for all her essentials. Your instincts were on high-alert from the day she was born, and you knew how to provide food, warmth, protection, assistance, kindness, understanding, direction, and most of all, love. All the cuteness and smiles she gave back helped you to feel confident that you were doing a good job.

Now she's changing, and you find it much more challenging to know how to provide the right amount of direction and information along with the necessary doses of affirmation.

What are the rites of passage that you will most likely celebrate during her first twenty years, besides birthdays? There's graduation from high school and . . . not much else. Sometimes family and friends offer up a cheer over her driver's license, when she is accepted by her desired university, or hired for a job she wanted. Do any of those moments reflect a true transition from childhood to adulthood?

No. Not the way that a young girl's *menarche* moves her from one side of childhood to the other side. Menarche comes from the Greek for "beginning" and refers to a girl's first period. This event occurs for every woman in every corner of the world and has since the beginning of time. It is healthy, normal, and natural. Yet it also largely remains shrouded in silence in Western culture.

In most families it falls to the parents, particularly the mom, to handle all the aspects of her daughter's menarche. That's why you want to be the one who initiates the impor–tant, confidence-building, and necessary conversation with your daughter.

I know moms who entered in by launching the conversa-tion and orchestrating something special to make this time of change memorable. I also know moms who relinquished

Life doesn't come with a manual, it comes with a mother.

their position when they approached this crossroad and let others become the more influential voices in their daughters' lives.

The moms who entered in, no matter how awkwardly or ill-prepared, all told me they're glad they did. For some, it took a new sort of courage, and I applaud them for being brave and creative. Many found it wasn't as daunting as they had imagined it would be.

As for the moms who told me they missed the moment, I wish you could see their faces. They're frustrated and dis-couraged. Most of them said they simply put it off and waited too long. They didn't set aside time for an impactful conver-sation. Many said they were too locked up in the shame of their own past to see how they might make their daughter's experience different and better than theirs was. Those moms lowered their eyes and said, "I wish I could go back to that time in my daughter's life and do it differently."

If you're one those moms, take heart. It's not too late. You can and should do something special now. Initiate a celebration. Start a new conversation. It's okay to tell her you wish you had done something sooner. Don't dwell on the delayed timing. Instead, focus on establishing the foundation now for many future conversations.

It's never too late to do something meaningful that says to your daughter, "I see you. I love you. I want to affirm you as a woman."

Your Responsibility

I live in Hawaii, and one of the words that's often used in daily conversations here is *kuleana*. The simple meaning in English is "responsibility."

Like most Hawaiian words, kuleana goes deeper than a singular meaning and has several layers. Kuleana depicts a symbiotic relationship in which a person recognizes the value of what they have to offer. Next, they make a choice to be generous and openly give what they have because they understand how it will benefit others. Their action is their unique kuleana.

That's a very different motivation than seeing a responsibility as your duty and gritting your teeth while doing what you must do, just to see it through.

As a mom, your kuleana with your daughter is to first see your worth and your place in your symbiotic relationship with her. Understand that what you have to offer is valuable. Then choose to generously give what you have as an act of love because it will benefit her.

Sharing and celebrating the mysteries of womanhood with your daughter should be a heart-to-heart gift you're giving her. It's not merely a chore that you're stuck with because you are her mother.

I hope you see your worth. I hope you feel motivated to take on your kuleana with much love.

"She is more precious than rubies."
Proverbs 31:10b, NLT

Stories from Other Moms and Daughters

Make It Fun

My mom had a way of adding fun to everything. When I started to "blossom," as she called it, she took my sister and me on a surprise shopping trip to a high-end retail store. We had an appointment with a personal stylist who put us in a large, fancy dressing room. She measured us for our accurate bra sizes even though my sister didn't need one yet. Then she brought a bunch of bras and bathing suits for us to try on. We had so much fun! I think that since it was such a posh setup and we were all doing it together, I didn't feel any sense of embarrassment. I loved being included with my mom in such a womanly, grown-up way.

One of the best things that happened was that the stylist kept saying that I had an "elegant long torso." I was eleven, and if you'd asked me to describe my figure, I would have said I was too tall, had big feet, and my rearend was abnormally flat. I knew how I compared to other girls my age, and to be honest, I'd never felt pretty until that day. Our stylist was sophisticated and beautiful. She made it seem as if my straight, long torso was an enviable feature.

I was different when I came home that day, wearing my first bra. I felt feminine and lovely. It was as if I'd been initiated into a special club and somehow my elegant long torso helped me to qualify as an above-average young lady.

Oh, the Possibilities!

What are some ways that you might put the thoughts from this chapter into action? What portions of the chapter stood out to you?

Here's a list of possible points of action:

• Pause right now to thank God for the children He has given you.

• Settle into your kuleana and accept your role in your daughter's life.

• Determine that you will do something special to usher your daughter into womanhood.

• Decide how and when you are going to set up your first "now that you're growing up" conversation.

• Ask other moms what they did when their daughters were young.

• Start a list of ideas gleaned from those women and add to it from the ideas in this book.

NOTES

Learn Her Language

When a woman is talking to you,
listen to what she says with her eyes.

Victor Hugo

Chapter Three

Learn Her Language

Have you noticed how our children can be just like us in some ways and, at the same time, completely different? Our daughters are not mini me's. They are not small clones who need to be taught how to become more like us. They are uniquely crafted individuals who are of immense value just the way God made them—as are we.

I have often wondered if a hint of that truth isn't embedded in Proverbs 22:6 (NASB).

> **Train up a child in the way he should go,**
> **even when he is old he will not depart from it.**

The wording, "the way they should go," seems to point to a child's unique makeup with a nudge toward them becoming fully who God created them to be. It doesn't say, "Train up a child in the way you went." Or "in the opposite way you went."

Every human is created to live a unique life. The training responsibility is on us as parents, but I see in this verse an emphasis on understanding exactly who our children are and what is essential for them to be prepared to fulfill their places in the world.

How do you learn your daughter's language? I have a few suggestions:

- Become a keen observer.
- Ask nonthreatening questions.
- Listen to the answers as well as the added hints of the deeper answers.
- Observe her expression and body language.
- Remember.

You must use your best detective skills to catch all the little clues. You must pause to ask questions so you can gather the key pieces to the mystery that is your child. You must be willing to adjust your expectations and discover what form of communication has the most value to your daughter.

Speaking your daughter's language means you are taking the time to tune in to her. It also communicates that you want to spend time with her because you value what she thinks and feels and has to say. You respect the things that are important in her world.

The Listening Language

When my kids were teens, I stumbled into learning a

brand new language that I called the Listening Language. I found that when our son and daughter came home from school, they didn't want twenty questions. On days when they did have something to share, they would start to tell me about it. But, without realizing it, I kept squelching the moment. I did this by interrupting, asking too many questions, and jumping in with advice they never asked for.

I caught myself doing this one day and determined that the next time they wanted to talk, I'd keep quiet. I'd pay attention. I'd make it clear that I was listening.

One day, when our son came home and started talking about something surprising that happened at school, I implemented my plan. The only sounds that came from my lips were delivered with calmness. Here's the vocabulary of the Listening Language that I developed that day:

Hmmm.

Oh.

Mmm-hmm.

I see.

Wow.

Really?

Uh-huh.

Your body language must coincide with the words. Focus on your relaxed posture, eye contact, understanding smiles, and eyebrows that rise or fall in sync with what you're hearing. It's a symphony of communication, and the two of you are the only instruments playing your unique song. Your role at the start is to provide the noninvasive, subtle background rhythm that gives the music structure and foundation but doesn't overshadow all the high and low notes.

The golden moment comes when your child finishes a

purge of the situation, having received only the listening language sounds and expressions from you. Then they relax slightly and extend an invitation for you to speak into the moment. Maybe they're just being polite. But if they ask for your input, most likely they sincerely want to hear what you have to say.

Now, be prepared to respond in a way that keeps the communication going. Refrain from saying what you've been dying to blurt out from the beginning. Instead, help your child give herself her own best advice by asking these three questions:

1. How do you feel about all that?
2. What do you think should happen next?
3. What are you going to do?

These simple questions can lead to some of the deepest, most complex conversations you'll have with your daughter, as she develops both her logic and communication skills. By using only the Listening Language during her waterfall of expression, you might well have earned the chance to take the topic deeper. I think you'll find that those three questions will keep the exchange going rather than turning the moment into a chance for you to stand at the pulpit and deliver your best sermon.

You might be surprised at how quickly the floodgates open when you ask the first question, "How do you feel about all that?" In some cases, that might be the only question you need to ask because a good cry and a warm hug could be all she needed from you.

The second question is often the most jarring. "What do you think should happen next?" This has the potential of becoming a blaring trumpet call to justice from her wounded heart. "I think she should apologize to me for what she said!" Or "I think the teacher should give me an extra day to finish because my project partner was sick."

That's why the third question is so important. When you ask, "What are you going to do?" you are rolling the decision-making power back on her. Even if her answer is, "I want you to tell me what-to-do," it's a victory because she's inviting you in.

Isn't it interesting that the pathway to becoming the most significant voice in your daughter's world is through a conversation that begins with you keeping your lips closed? You are a filter as well as an instructor and have been since before she was born. The rhythm of your communication changes in every season.

When you're ready to take the Listening Language from the initial "you—me" phase into the "us" phase, you'll need to find something you both like.

Shared Loves

My daughter and I love *Anne of Green Gables*. You, too? Oh, good. Then you'll understand why this became such a fun shared love for us.

We discovered the Sullivan Entertainment version of the film series when Rachel was in second grade. I bought the series starring Megan Follows as Anne, and my daughter and I instituted our annual "Anne with an 'E' Day" that lasted into her college years. On the last day of school each year, which was usually a half-day, when Rachel arrived at home, I would have everything set up. She and I would have the TV reserved for the next six hours.

Our Anne with an "E" Day was an interactive experience. When Anne and Diana did their three-legged race at the church picnic, we tied our legs together and skittered around the island in the kitchen. As Anne prepared her special tea party for Diana (who was "sampling" the raspberry cordial), we sipped cherry juice from my aunt's special crystal glasses and nibbled on small, triangular, crustless sandwiches.

We crossed our arms with Anne and closed our eyes as she boarded the borrowed rowboat and arranged her long hair to look like the Lady of Shallot. When Matthew collapsed in the field, Rachel and I always reached for the Kleenex at the same time, every time. We stood straight and tall in a show of camaraderie at the recital of "The Highwayman." With Anne, we chanted, "When the moon is a ghostly galleon tossed upon cloudy seas. . . "

By my estimation, we did this for eleven years. It became "our thing."

One year my daughter wanted to include a friend, who came over with her mother and her sister. They didn't get it when we clomped around the kitchen's island in the three-legged race. They didn't care for the cherry juice. Nor did they even make it to the scene with Anne and Gilbert on the bridge when, Rachel and I always leaned our heads on each other's shoulders and swooned, "Oh, Gilbert Blythe!" It wasn't Rachel's friend's thing—nor her mother's or sister's.

It was our thing, and we never invited them or anyone else to join us again. This became one of our shared loves. Just for us.

The surprise was how some exceptionally good conversations about boys, careers, and death flowed out of our annual Anne with an "E" Day. Anne's stories initiated conversations about real life, and I've always been grateful for those free-flowing talks.

Take a moment now to think about something that you and your daughter both like. Think about how you can take steps to make it your thing. Your shared love. Start by considering the natural times when your interests overlap such as baking, crafting, sports, shopping, music, or travel. Having something just the two of you enjoy and creating your own traditions around it will bond you in sweet and fun ways.

Promises Kept

Another aspect of learning your daughter's language involves making and keeping a promise of some form of celebration when she enters puberty. The trust you'll build with her in this process is more important than it might appear at first glance. Don't let uncertainty hamper you. Go ahead and promise her something to celebrate when puberty occurs.

For instance, has she been asking to have her ears pierced? If that's something you've agreed to and have been saying, "Not now but one day," why not promise that when she starts her period, you'll go together to have her ears pierced. Make it a shared, fun, just-us moment.

Does she want to wear makeup like an older sister or a friend at school? Promise that you'll set up an appointment for her with a beauty specialist. Let the professional show her the best way to care for her skin and apply age-appropriate makeup.

When you create a shared experience around the fun of wearing cosmetics, she will be less likely to sneak a tube of mascara into her backpack and take lessons from girls in the mirror of the school bathroom.

Lots of moms told me stories of their promises kept, including overnight trips to a hotel, conference, or retreat. Their daughter's love language was quality time, which meant they valued the shared time together away from the usual routine at home. If you plan a getaway, and it happens to be linked to business or other commitments you have, make sure that your responsibilities don't rob the two of you of lots of free time together.

I spoke at a women's retreat recently during which a teen girl kept hanging around the book table. She wanted to talk and talk and talk to me. I finally asked if she was going to do any of the planned free-time activities, such as the crafts or hike. She said, "I only came because my mom said we would do things together. But when we got here, she volunteered to help in the kitchen."

The teen told me she tried to help in the kitchen, too, but the other women told her to leave and find something fun to do. Apparently, lengthy conversations with me about her girl's softball team was the only thing she could find to do. I felt sad for her. The promise was hollow. I also felt for her mom because the next time she suggested that she and her thirteen-year-old have a girls' weekend, you know that teenager is not going to be interested. Speaking your daughter's language means you are taking the time to tune in to her because you value what she thinks, feels, and has to say.

No act of kindness no matter how small is ever wasted.
Aesop

Stories from Other Moms and Daughters

Treat Her Like a Lady

When I was growing up, I was such a tomboy that I shopped in the men's department. I was an athlete and wanted clothes that let me move. I had no interest in tea parties and pretty little ponies. My mom is artistic, generous, and creative. When I turned sixteen, she gave me a pair of pearl earrings in a velvet jewelry box and said, "Every woman needs a pair of pearl earrings."

My response was, "Heeey. . .thaaanks?"

I got the impression that those earrings were my mom's way of saying, "Welcome to the Woman Club." They pointed to the other side of the tomboy years and shaped my view of what was yet to come.

Even though I didn't fit the stereotype of what femininity looked like among the other young girls in my generation, I am so glad that my mom affirmed my identity as a woman during my teen years. I wasn't confused about the way God created me because my mom made it clear that it was okay to be a strong, capable, no-frills, athletic woman. That didn't change anything. I was still fully female. Her gift of the pearls instilled a sense of a greater femininity that was yet to be awakened in my life.

My favorite part of the story is how my relationship

with my mom grew closer as I grew older. When I married, I asked my mom to be my matron of honor. And yes, of course, I wore the pearls on my wedding day. Now that my husband and I have two children, I plan to continue the tradition with our daughter.

Oh, the Possibilities!

What are some ways that you might put the thoughts from this chapter into action? What portions of the chapter stood out to you?

Here's a list of possible points of action:

1. Practice the Listening Language.

2. Discover your "shared love." Don't worry about how many attempts you have to make before one of them clicks for both of you.

3. Set up something special for just the two of you and establish it as a tradition.

4. Prepare a special gift for your daughter, such as a family heirloom piece of jewelry, for when she enters puberty.

NOTES

Make Your Plan

Mothers hold their children's hands for a short while but their hearts forever.

Author Unknown

Chapter Four

Make Your Plan

Is your creative mind humming with ideas of what would work well with your daughter? Good! Now, let me help you make your plan.

For those of you who love checklists, here's what we will chat about in this section. I started with the "don'ts" and then went on to the "do's."

Don't:

• Wait too long before you set up a special time with your daughter

• Assume others are going to do your job for you

• Think that one size fits all

Do:

• Plan ahead and be intentional about setting up a special time and place

• See this as a celebration

• Prepare yourself and your words ahead of time

The next question is, what style will work best for your girl and you? Fuss/no fuss? Group/no group?

You'll find some stories and suggestions for each of these approaches in this chapter, but first I want to emphasize the most important ingredient of all will be your full attention. Whatever you do, make sure the moments are marked by eye contact, soft smiles, and unhurried words.

She might not want you to hold her hand anymore, but this is your chance to assure her that she can trust you to hold her heart.

Your daughter knows the difference between when you're merely present and when you are all there. Let her know you only have eyes for her. You want to be with her. She can take all the time in the world to process the conversation and ask as many questions as she wants. No phones. No distractions. Full attention.

When you have that strategy in mind from the beginning, this conversation will be set apart from all the comings and goings and partial conversations of a normal day. For many moms, who often feel they are in survival mode and life keeps rolling from one urgency to another, being intentional and focused during a set aside time with your preteen will be a gift to her in and of itself. I think you'll find that time will be a gift for you, as well.

Your objective for this personal conversation is to establish that you care about her, you are available to her, and since you are on the other side of all these changes, you want to be the one who says to her, "Welcome to womanhood."

What's the best way to do that? Think about her last birthday party or comments she made about a recent event or a friend's birthday. Did she want lots of friends to come or just do something simple and quiet? Does she love to come up with special gifts for friends and family? How much does she like to enter into the hoopla of decorating for Christmas or other holidays? These will be your best clues to know if she's a fuss/no fuss kind of girl or a group/no group sort of young woman.

The examples in the rest of this chapter will also help you to clarify what your girl would like best so you can start putting your plan into motion with confidence.

Fuss

My daughter was all about the fuss and frills. As I mentioned earlier, I knew the best thing I could do for her would be to set up a private party at home for just the two of us and bring out our china teacups.

I set the date and made sure it was a time when my husband and son would be out of the house. I created a very girly invitation and sealed the envelope with a heart sticker. The invitation waited for her on her pillow the day before the party.

Rachel was all in. While she was at school the next day, I went to a bakery and bought a mini-cake that had four layers and was topped with pink rosebuds. I prepared a special gift

You Are
Invited

bag for her with tissue paper fluffed out at the top. Inside was a small box of panty liners, a travel-size bottle of body spray, a miniature bar of her favorite chocolate, and a tube of watermelon-flavored lip balm.

When Rachel came home from school, she went to her room to get ready. We lived in the Northwest at the time, and the rainy weather meant we usually wore jeans and sweaters for nine months of the year. On that cold January afternoon I had the fire going. Mellow music floated through the house. The coffee table was set with my favorite teapot, china teacups, the yummy-looking cake, a tiny bouquet of flowers, and her gift bag. I even found sugar cubes decorated with pink flowers.

All the frills.

I heard Rachel's bedroom door open and looked up from the couch to see her at the top of the stairs wearing her favorite dress-up gown, a pale blue, flowing bridesmaid's dress I had worn at my sister's wedding. She floated down the stairs with a grace all her own and sat beside me on the couch. I loved her expression as she took in the gift bag and the sweets.

"This is all for you," I said as I cut the cake. "I wanted to celebrate you!"

"Why?"

I poured the tea, and we stirred in the sugar cubes and cream.

"I wanted to celebrate you because your body is beginning to change, and I wanted to be the first one to welcome you to womanhood." I held up my teacup, and she lifted hers. We sat together like fine ladies as I told her the ancient mystery of how her body would change and what would happen next. With teary-eyed sincerity, I explained that God made a woman's body to carry, nurture, and deliver new life. This was a privilege not given to men. Only to women.

"And not even to angels," Rachel added.

I paused. "That's true. Not even angels can have babies. Only women."

Her wide, blue eyes didn't blink. "It's an honor to be a woman, then, isn't it?"

Her comment caught me off guard. I'm not sure I had ever considered my femaleness to be an honor. I felt my throat tightening as I realized what a completely different attitude and response my daughter was having than I had when the realities of puberty were being revealed. Shame would not be an heirloom passed down to her. (I'll tell you more about my story later.)

Rachel opened her gift bag. A casual explanation followed of how to best use the panty liners. I wanted her to know she had the freedom to use them every day if it helped her feel confident and prepared. She tried out the lip balm and gave her bare arm a spritz of the strawberry-scented body spray.

I invited her to ask questions. She had a few. Mostly she wanted to understand both male and female organs and body parts. I hadn't expected that and wasn't prepared by having any pamphlets or books on hand.

We went up to my bedroom, and I pulled an old biology textbook from my dusty bookshelves. She and I cuddled up on the bed, and the conversation continued as we looked at the medical journal-type illustrations together. It felt natural to point to the labeled body parts and explain how a husband and wife bring their bodies together.

Going into the specifics felt more comfortable than I thought it would be. The pictures helped. It's a good idea to gather whatever resource materials you need ahead of time so that you'll feel prepared as the conversation continues.

Rachel and I went back downstairs to the romantic setting with the fire, the remaining sweets, and the soft music. Through the front windows we saw that it had begun to snow. The fluffy snowflakes seemed to flutter in the glow of the streetlight, like tiny ivory ballerinas wearing gilded slippers.

Rachel reached for my hands and said the words she had been uttering since she was a toddler. "Come on, Mom. Let's dance."

We twirled and sashayed, dipped, and swayed in response to the background music, smiling at each other eye-to-eye, heart-to-heart. Neither of us will ever forget that enchanting moment.

The song ended, and to conclude our little holy hullabaloo, I placed the palm of my hand on her forehead and blessed her with a familiar nighttime blessing her dad and I had spoken over both our kids since they were little.

May the Lord bless you and keep you.
May the Lord make His face shine upon you
And give you His peace.
And may you always love Jesus
more than anything else.

We adapted the blessing from the ancient verses in Numbers 6:24-26. Rachel received the blessing with her eyes closed and her lips upturned with a contented smile. I leaned closer and whispered, "Welcome to womanhood, my darling girl."

Just telling you about this warms me all over again. The time was powerful, peaceful, and generational-altering for both of us. I can honestly say that up until that day, I had never thanked God for the annoyance of monthly periods. I had never felt grateful for the way my body did what it was supposed to do.

Rachel changed the way I thought about menstruation that day because she was right. It is an honor to be a woman.

No Fuss

If you and your daughter have a no-frills way of connecting and you know that she would be nauseous if you bought a teapot and told Siri to play airy-fairy harp music, here's a completely different scenario for you.

A friend told me about the "It's an Honor to be a Woman" Day she stumbled onto with her eight-year-old daughter. I think she did a great job of sailing through the moment with little fuss but lots of open doors for communication. Here's what happened.

Her daughter sidled up to her in the kitchen one afternoon and spilled a distressing bit of info she had heard on the playground and asked if it was true.

My friend stopped everything, looked her innocent first-born in the eyes, and said, "The part that's true is that your body is going to change in a few years. The part that's not true is what you heard about bleeding to death."

Her daughter looked only slightly comforted, so my friend said, "Start thinking about all the questions you have about what you heard, and let's talk about it when you go to bed tonight."

That night, when her daughter was settled in the safe familiarity of her room, my friend sat on her daughter's bed. "Before you ask your questions, I want to read you some verses I've always liked." She read Psalm 139:13 from (TLB).

You made all the delicate, inner parts of my body
and knit them together in my mother's womb.

Placing her palm on her lower abdomen, she said, "This is where my womb is. This is where God knit you together inside of me. Since you're a girl like me, you have a womb, too. It's also called a uterus."

From there, she explained how a lining of blood builds up each month to prepare a cushioned place for a baby to grow someday. The body knows each month that since no baby is in there, the lining isn't needed so it slowly flows out of the woman's body.

It wasn't a lot of information, but it was enough. The fear of bleeding to death was removed. The other gruesome things she had heard at school were resolved after several questions, and her daughter's eight-year-old imagination was satisfied and relieved that it would be a few more years before she would have her first period.

The no-fuss approach allowed the conversation to start, and now they could keep adding details that fit with her daughter's age and ability to understand.

I especially like two of the things my friend did. She stopped everything and addressed her daughter's questions eye-to-eye but shifted the longer conversation to when she knew they wouldn't be interrupted and could keep the communication going privately.

I also liked that she started the conversation in her daughter's bedroom by reading a verse. She brought the sense of the sacred to their time by revealing what God has to say about the human body, thus elevating the schoolyard talk to a topic that should be respected.

Group

Do you think your girl would relish a group event that honors preteen girls? I heard from several women who host gatherings like this. One of them called theirs the "Girls Are Amazing" party and held it each year for the fifth-grade girls at their church.

The benefit of honoring all the young girls at the same time with a special event is that there's power in combining the voices of all the mentors who speak into their lives that night. One of the speakers might be an expert in fashion and can demonstrate how to put together outfits that are mom-approved, work well on a young girl's changing shape, and yet still look cute and current. This can be a big help for moms who are fighting an uphill battle over what their blossoming daughters want to wear.

Another woman might share an inspirational message that incorporates truths from God's Word in a way that communicates directly to a preadolescent's heart and mind. I'm so grateful for the teachers, speakers, and mentors my daughter admired when she was growing up. They were able to say exactly what I'd been trying to say but in a role-model way that caused Rachel to remember what they talked about. More than once she would repeat to me things they suggested, and I would think, "Hey, I've been saying that for years."

All moms sound like white noise to their daughters at some point. Sad, but true. That's why we should be grateful for the other women, the other voices who speak truth to our daughters in a way they can hear and take to heart. Instead of being jealous of those influential voices, let's thank God for them.

I read about an entrepreneurial mom in Atlanta who started "Period Parties" and now offers them to others. She facilitates a fun event that includes a panel of savvy women who discuss topics such as irregular periods, hormones and conversation starters for both boys and girls. All women are welcome. Many of the moms who attend have more than one daughter and appreciate having a group event they can all go to.

One of the bonuses of your daughter attending a gathering where all the facets of growing up are discussed is that it will help her to feel included. She becomes part of an elite bunch who were the guests of honor at a special party. Since other friends also receive the same information, this can help draw them closer as they grow up together.

Make sure that you don't slide into a mentality of checking "the talk" off your list and think everything your daughter needs to know was covered at the event. The purpose of the group event is to start the conversation. It still falls on you as her mom to capture that singular, "Welcome to Womanhood" moment between just the two of you. Your time together will give her a chance to ask any questions she's been pondering and give you a chance to build on the party's theme about how special women's bodies are and how we can respect them.

You'll be at a disadvantage if you drop your daughter off at the church event, pick her up the next morning, and never enter into a deeper conversation with her. Consider the event to be an invitation to step into your daughter's life and keep the conversation going from there on.

No Group

If a large group event isn't a possibility or a preference for your daughter and you, what about aiming for the no-group approach by setting up a special time for just the two of you? Or, keep it small and include one close friend.

I know two moms who are close friends. They both had daughters who were the same age, and the girls had been best friends since they were toddlers. The girls became as close as sisters. As they approached puberty, the moms decided to do something special together since their daughters were inseparable.

They planned a luncheon for the four of them and reserved one of the tables in a restaurant's private, small room. In a lovely, grown-up way, the daughters were treated like young ladies as the moms took turns sharing the details of puberty and tag-teaming as they answered questions.

The daughters also tag-teamed with their questions, and the conversation easily rolled into other topics, which made the time feel full and varied.

One of the best results of this approach was that the girls had each other to talk with on a deeper level, since neither of them had sisters. Sometimes a girl needs someone other than her mom to go to; the luncheon confirmed that they had another mom who cared about them and was available during the growing-up years, too.

As you make your plan for the best way to celebrate with your daughter, be kind to yourself. Don't overthink it. There's no exact right or wrong way to do this. If you have several daughters, you already know that your plan will vary with each of them. Don't worry about being fair or equal. Focus on the individual needs of each daughter.

The objective is for you to try. To make an effort. To show that you care. That's the message that will come through no matter what approach you take or how "successful" your attempt turns out. This is an ongoing conversation. You can add to it at any time. Just make sure to start the conversation.

Stories from Other Moms and Daughters

The Gift of Written Words

My mom did something thoughtful when I started my period. She and I are a lot alike, and she knew that all I'd want to do was hide in my room. She brought me a cup of cocoa with a toasted English muffin with honey (my favorite comfort food) and the hot water bottle. Then she handed me a small stack of envelopes tied with a green polka-dotted ribbon, again, my favorite.

I got comfortable and opened the cards that were from the women in our large family. My mom had asked each of them to write me a private note with some advice on becoming a woman. One of my aunts, who is really beautiful, included a faded Polaroid from when she was my age. I never would have recognized her! She was gangly and had braces, and her hair was wild.

In her letter she wrote, "What you believe on the inside will soon take over the outside. I believe you are beautiful. What do you believe?"

Every letter had a similar gem. I felt as if the women in my family had crafted an invisible crown for me with all their shining words. I read their letters many times during my teen years and kept them in a special box in my closet. Each time I read them, I felt as if their advice and blessings were giving me courage and renewed compassion for myself and for others.

I'm 28 now, and two of the women who contributed to my mom's project have passed. That makes the gift of their words to me in their handwriting more treasured than ever.

A letter is . . .
such a faithful copy of the beloved voice which speaks,
that fragile souls count it
among love's most precious treasures.

Honoré de Balzac

Oh, the Possibilities!

What are some ways that you might put the thoughts from this chapter into action? What portions of the chapter stood out to you?

Here's a list of possible points of action:

• Figure out if your daughter is a fuss/no fuss, group/no group girl

• Come up with a few ideas of what you want to do for her or with her

• Reach out to whomever you need to partner with you to make it happen

• Don't delay. Get what you need and have it ready before the time comes to bless her

NOTES

Normalize Respect

May our daughters be like stately columns
which adorn the corners of a palace.

Psalm 144:12b, GNT

Chapter Five

Normalize Respect

Our family attended a wedding reception some years ago during which one of the guests came up to where we were standing with his wife. He spoke to her in a derogatory way and then reached for her breast, squeezed it in front of all of us, and walked off, saying he was going to get a piece of wedding cake. His wife let out a twittering laugh and a shrug. "Boys will be boys."

I was in shock. My grown son looked like a statue. Only his eyes moved to catch my gaze. My expression must have looked like I was in pain because later, when my husband and I talked with our son about it, he said I looked like I was going to cry.

"I did feel like I was about to cry," I said. "No woman should ever be treated that way. Especially by her husband and in public!"

What followed was a long family conversation on respect and honor. My husband and I got an education on how our kids' peers talk to each other and treat each other at school. My heart ached to think of how much our culture has disintegrated and how rare it is to be shown courtesy and honor.

I broke into full-on lecture mode because I felt desperate for my young-adult children to understand what normal and acceptable behavior is, regardless of what they've seen elsewhere. I told them I expected them to go against the flow and to consistently be respectful of others as well as their own bodies and to accept nothing less than that from anyone.

From that revealing conversation, I became convinced that moms in this generation have an even greater responsibility to instill a sense of honor and respect in their sons and daughters. It's not a quality that is perpetuated in their circles or in our culture in general.

When a young woman respects herself, she makes decisions and takes action from a place of strength and dignity rather than shrugging off the unacceptable behavior of others.

> *Strength and dignity are her clothing,*
> *and she smiles at the future.*
> Proverbs 31:25, NASB

What does it take to normalize respect?

It takes parents who start the conversation with their children at a young age and keep it going as they grow older and are exposed to more outside influences. Begin with your daughter now, at whatever age she is, and help her to understand her value. Teach her how she should be treated.

I've always liked the imagery in the blessing in Psalm 144:12 that appears at the beginning of this chapter. When we raise our daughters to be like strong pillars or stately columns, they become the women who hold up "palaces." They stand firm with strength and beauty. They are the structural pillars that keep families, businesses, and communities held in place. Their distinct beauty is the first thing a visitor notices. Without their powerful support, the structure would crumble.

So don't mess with my beautiful pillar of a daughter. Strength and dignity are her clothing. She has reason to smile at the future.

Your Conversation Plan

How can you protect your daughter's innocence and at the same time prepare her for the adult world? Respect is essential, and so is open communication. Keep doing all the things you're doing now to filter out the harmful influences. Protect her imagination.

At the same time, always keep the conversation door unlocked so she can come to you when she's presented with unknown words, images, and information. Settle on language that feels comfortable to both of you ahead of time.

I remember when our son came in from playing with neighborhood kids and tried out a new word he had just heard. Trust me, the word should not be included in any nine-year-old's vocabulary. I asked if he knew what it meant. He said no, but the other boys laughed so he repeated it, and they laughed again.

Instead of explaining the word's crude meaning, I told

him the word described a disrespectful way to treat another person. I chose not to give any anatomical facts or explanations because I wanted to protect his imagination. I told him our family wouldn't use that term and the other boys laughed because they knew it was a disrespectful thing to say.

My son seemed satisfied with my explanation, and the rest of our conversation turned to how important it is to show respect to others.

When I thought about it later, I was glad I hadn't automatically used the terms "dirty" or "nasty." There's nothing dirty or nasty about God's creation. Reproduction in all its forms is miraculous because it came from God.

When God made stars, whales, and daffodils, He said they were "good." When God made humans—man and woman/male and female—He said they were "very good." Our bodies are part of the "very good" of God's creation. We are elevated above the animals, the elements, and the Earth. Our bodies are meant to be shared in gloriously delightful ways within the sacred gift of marriage.

One of the ways you'll protect your daughter's innocence as well as her imagination is not to refer to any part of the human body as nasty. Elevate conversations by expressing respect for every human body. Emphasize all that is honorable and make sure she only hears you refer to anything sexual with respect.

Body Image

This might be an uncomfortable topic for you. I hope you'll keep reading because if you can get to where you're comfortable talking about your body in a respectful way, it will set the tone for a better future for your daughter and her self-image.

For some women, just thinking about respect, appropriate touching, and self-protection can trigger painful memories. If you are one of those women, I understand. When those painful memories come rushing back, they can bring a mental and emotional paralysis from childhood or young-adult experiences. The assigned task of speaking about these things to your daughter can feel overwhelming.

Please be gentle with yourself. Take this topic step-by-step. I want you to be able to move forward and experience the healing God can infuse into your life.

If you've never addressed deep issues of abuse, shame, self-hatred, and injustice, I urge you to seek counsel. Tell your story to a trusted and qualified counselor.

Set your heart on being healed and whole.

I went to a skilled Christian counselor when our children were almost teens and was surprised at what poured out of my heart during the first few sessions. I'd gone to a medical doctor first, and he diagnosed my symptoms as premenopausal. I went on a search for natural aides to balance my hormones but found that talking through my old, nagging issues had a valuable, stabilizing effect.

The counselor delivered truth that both hurt and helped and I remember going home after one of the sessions feeling exhausted. For many years, whenever difficult times hit me, I would go on a hunt to find hope and courage in God's Word. This time, Philippians 3:13 (TLB) became an anchor for my floundering thoughts and emotions.

I am still not all I should be, but I am bringing all my energies to bear on this one thing: Forgetting the past and looking forward to what lies ahead.

After completing a series of sessions with the counselor, the physical and emotional anxieties began to lift. I saw all the pieces of my past that I had labeled as broken and unusable as being something beautiful because they came out of the redeemable heap of humanity that all of us experience in some way or other. Those broken shards, with their irregular edges, had been shaped through the breaking experiences.

By taking them out of hiding and putting them all out on the table like puzzle pieces, the counselor was soldering them together with my life as it was now. All the fractured pieces had a place. My life now told a story. A story with no shame.

We are so familiar with the darkness. We are good at hiding, you and I. Retreating is as old as Adam and Eve. Remember how they went into hiding in the Garden of Eden? Their first instinct was to withdraw, to cover up, to try to remedy their own shame and not to be seen or known.

That didn't stop God from coming to them, seeking them, and calling out, "Where are you?"

I believe God still comes walking in the cool of the evening through the garden of our hearts and calls out the same question to us: "Where are you?"

Adam answered that he was ashamed, and so they hid. The relationship Adam and Eve had with God could move forward when they came out of hiding, talked about what had happened, and received what God had for them in the next season of their lives.

I've seen this pattern repeated many times over the years

in my relationship with God. I mess up, I get messed up, I feel strangled by shame, and I go into hiding. I hide from people and from God.

The moment I come out of hiding and confess, open up, tell the truth, and draw near to God is when I take steps on a redemptive path that leads out of darkness into light. The result always has led to freedom. Always.

The light shining through the soldered-together pieces of our stained-glass lives always tells a story. It's a one-of-a-kind God story of how everything is redeemable. Something beautiful can be made from the broken shards.

I dearly want you to walk in freedom as you come alongside your daughter and lead her into this next season of her life. I want you to feel a sense of dignity and restored respect for your own body as well as hers as you move forward.

Establishing a foundation of respect will affect every conversation you have with your daughter, which is why I believe it needs to be in place before rolling into details with her on how her body is changing.

Essentials for Self-Respect

You can start at any age to instill a sense of value and self-respect in your daughter. I realize that some of you moms are much more high detail than I am, and you may have already come up with ten essential topics you want to cover with your daughter before she's ten. But the two respect-inducing topics I've listed below are a starting point, if you have no such list.

Just make sure you don't overwhelm or overeducate your daughter in an attempt to be thorough. Pay attention to how she responds. Only answer the questions she asks, not the ones she hasn't yet considered. Move ahead at her pace, even if you're well-supplied with information and suggestions.

1. Her amazing body

• Even as a toddler, she can understand from books and educational shows how intricately God has made us. Is she curious about how the lungs work? Fascinated by hearing her heartbeat through a stethoscope? Nurture her curiosity.

• Nurture the wonder of her body. Tell her how strong her arms are, what pretty fingers she has, and how much you love her smile. Compliment her and help her come to love features that someone else pointed out in a negative way.

• Use anatomically correct terms for body parts because this conveys respect. Slang terms are demeaning.

• Express a sense of acceptance and appreciation for your own body. Being kind to yourself in front of her teaches a powerful lesson without a single lecture on self-esteem. Show rather than just tell your daughter how a woman should feel about herself.

2. Her privacy

• Experts say that a good general guideline for children is to tell them that no one may touch or see the parts of their body that would be covered by underwear or a bathing suit.

• Assure your daughter that she has every right to defend and protect herself if her privacy feels threatened or if someone attempts to show disrespect toward her body. My husband taught our daughter self-defense moves when she was young. Blessedly, she never had to use them. But she was prepared to protect the privacy of her own body.

• Allow her the privacy of a closed door, a chance to be alone, space to cry, or to burn off steam before telling you what she's upset about.

You can cover these key conversation topics at any age. The sooner you begin, the easier it will be when the time comes to slide into deeper topics. Some conversations are freer flowing in the car. But for other conversations, you can place a higher value on the topic by being face-to-face so that you can both catch the nuances in your expressions. Talking about these essential topics will help her to see early on that she can talk with you about the important things in life and that the conversation will feel natural and respectful.

Respect Demonstrated in a Group

I mentioned in the previous chapter that some women put together a special event for all the fifth-grade girls at their church. The younger sisters couldn't wait until it was their turn to be invited to the "Girls Are Amazing" party.

The event included a sleepover with silly games, music, sleeping bags, and pj's along with lots of fun food and laughter. Several women that the girls looked up to came and gave short, fun talks on skin care, modesty, friendships, hygiene, and most importantly, what God has to say about their value.

In the morning they had a hands-on cooking class with a female chef who talked about healthy eating. The girls went home with a gift bag filled with easy, healthy recipes; shampoo samples; bookmarks with Bible verses; and a gift card to their local Christian bookstore.

The program was designed to be in tandem with what the girls' mothers were doing to prepare them for puberty. It wasn't designed to take the place of any of the important conversations a mom would have with her daughter but rather to be a positive side conversation that supported everything the parents were doing to make their daughter's journey into womanhood an exciting and honoring experience.

Again, it's all about starting with a foundation of respect. The women who put together the event honored the families, the girls, and that the process is different for each girl. Their mission was to create a welcoming community environment for the young girls and to give them positive affirmation that becoming a woman was an amazing adventure.

Wouldn't you have loved going to something like that when you were in fifth grade? I would have considered such an event to be the absolute best memory of my early adolescence.

I especially appreciate that the women who organized the gathering saw the importance of talking to the girls about their value in Christ. I've been writing for teen girls for decades and have received thousands of letters from readers. One consistent theme in those letters has been how the readers view God and their questions about how He views them.

They've shared many misconceptions with me. From young ages many of them become stuck on thinking that God is going to be mad at them if they don't do everything in life perfectly. Others have written to me about their lofty aspirations that failed and said, "I just wanted to make God and my parents proud of me."

To all those young women I want to say, "Shame off you. Grace on you."

Shame off you
Grace on you

I've included those words in many of my books and talks and have heard reactions from hundreds, maybe thousands of readers. Many of their comments kept coming to mind as I wrote a nonfiction study book for teen girls entitled *Spoken For*. I co-authored the book with Alyssa Bethke because we both wanted to find new ways to tell girls how valuable they are to God. He's not waiting with a lightning bolt to strike you when you sin. Nor is He waiting for you to do something heroic that will make Him proud of you.

God doesn't respond to our choices with clenched fists saying that He wants to "get you back." Instead, He responds with open arms and extended, nail-pierced hands because He wants to "get you back" and welcome you into His arms. His love is unfailing. It's many-faceted and beautifully tender.

In *Spoken For* I created a list entitled, "What God Says about You." I assembled verses from Genesis to Revelation in which God uses specific words that tell us exactly what He thinks about us and how He feels about us. You'll find that list at the end of this book.

If you are intentional about normalizing respect by teaching it and modeling it for your daughter, you will be amazed to see how self-confident she will become as she heads into puberty.

Stories from Other Moms and Daughters

When Dad Shares the Moments

Both my parents are reserved, but they did two things that made me feel as if they cared about me and respected my feelings during my early adolescent years.

First, they read through the entire Christy Miller High School series with me at night. They would take turns coming into my room at bedtime and reading a chapter. Sometimes we had to read two chapters because of the cliffhangers! They would ask me nonthreatening questions, like, "Do you know any guys like Todd?" or "What would you do if you were Christy and Alissa left you at the party?" Or "Do you have a friend who acts like Katie?"

We had the best conversations. I've always been grateful for that time with my parents and the way the fictional role models in the stories went through all the same things I went through with friends, first love, school, and my family. It was as if Christy's pretend story gave me an open door to talk to my parents about my real-life story.

The second thing my mom did well was to have "the talk" with me in a natural, almost scientific way. That's what felt most comfortable and respectful to her. When I started my period, I already had everything I needed, and I knew what was happening. I told my mom right away. She gave me a big hug and asked if it was okay with me if she told my dad. I said she could because it felt natural for him to be included in the moment.

That night my dad came home with a big bouquet of carnations for me. It was kind of like his way of reenacting the scene in *Summer Promise* when Todd gave Christy the carnations, but mine were pink. When he gave me the bouquet he said, "Now that you're a woman, I wanted to be the first man to give you flowers and tell you how much I love you."

It's one of my favorite childhood/young adulthood memories. My parents didn't need to say much. I knew I was loved, protected, and respected.

Oh, the Possibilities!

What are some ways that you might put the thoughts from this chapter into action? What portions of the chapter stood out to you?

Here's a list of possible points of action:

• Use the "What God Says about You" list at the end of this book to customize a study with your daughter. Underline each verse in your own Bibles when you read them together. You might want to read the surrounding verses ahead of time to get the full context.

• Ask her what words of loving affirmation from her Heavenly Father she sees in each of the verses. Be sure to listen to her first and then add your thoughts on how the verse affects the way you view yourself in light of how God sees you.

• If you're great at organizing, get together with some

other moms to plan your own version of a "Girls Are Amazing" party, large or small.

• Make a plan with your husband, mom, sister, or friend ahead of time and ask them to enter into the rite-of-passage moment with your daughter. They can do this by having a card or letter ready for you to hand to her or a small gift such as the idea of a bouquet from her dad. That way you're inviting the other important adults in your daughter's life to be part of an affirming circle.

NOTES

Celebrate the Moment

If you exalt wisdom, she will exalt you.
Hold her fast, and she will lead you to great honor;
she will place a beautiful crown upon your head.

Proverbs 4:8-9, TLB

Chapter Six

Celebrate the Moment

Time flies. We know that.

My question for you, dear caring mama, is what can you do to make time stop for one memorable moment? Instead of letting the wave of oncoming puberty wash over both of you with all its emotional, shore-pounding certainty, how can you take your daughter by the hand and dive in together?

Pause and think. Ask God for wisdom. From all the examples and ideas shared in the earlier chapters, hold on to the pieces that resonated with you. Dream a little right now. What can you do that would make your daughter feel celebrated and special?

I think it would help if we talked some more about celebrations. As I'm sure you've noticed, they aren't the same for everyone or for every occasion. It's challenging to get this one just right because chances are, you don't have a lot of previous coming-of-age celebrations to draw inspiration from.

Bestowing Gifts

For many women, young and old, it's not really a party unless gifts are involved. They don't see how their daughter will feel as if she's been celebrated unless a gift of a floral wreath is given to mark the moment, or a flurry of wrapping paper and expressions of surprise and delight are included.

That's how it was for the women in my novel *Becoming Us*, when ten-year-old Audra has her first period. Her mom organizes a small party with the women who are the most important in Audra's life. Each woman brings a small gift with a coming-of-age meaning attached to it.

For instance, Sierra gives her an assortment of flavored lip glosses and tells Audra that every single kiss has value and that's why a wise young woman saves those kisses and gives them away sparingly. Christy gives Audra a journal and tells her how helpful it was for Christy to write out all her thoughts and prayers when she was a teen.

At the end of the sweet, gift-giving time, Audra's mother crowns her with a wreath of flowers and tells her she is a daughter of the King of kings and always to remember who she is and whose she is.

Yes, the moment was created by me for a group of imaginary women. But I realized it was more than that when I heard from readers who set up the same sort of coming-of-age party for the young women in their lives, using the scene as their model.

As encouraging as that is, I also realize that some of you

are cringing as you read this because gift-giving is a challenge. I'm not an expert at gift-giving, but some of the women I'm closest to are. My daughter is a superb gift-giver. So is my sister. I just don't have that mindset. If you're like me, this is where you'll need to tune in to your daughter's love language.

Does she light up when she receives gifts? Or does quality time together turn on the conversation waterfall? Does she shower you with appreciation when you do something extra for her? If she thrives on words of affirmation, you'll want to make sure you give her plenty of praise. And if being close and cuddling is still her favorite position to be in with you, plan your conversation-starting moment accordingly. All of these are valuable ways to mark the moment.

With my daughter, Rachel, I realized at our living room tea party that the gift bag I had presented to her was more of a party favor than a true gift. When she was fourteen, she and I made plans for another special tea party. This time I bought her a ring that she had pointed out many times. We went to a luxurious tearoom for our celebration. When the waiter brought the three-tiered tea tray with the sweets and savories, I put my sneaky little plan into motion.

"Why don't we pray?" I suggested.

Rachel bowed her head and closed her eyes. As I was thanking God that we could enjoy this special time together, I slipped one of the cucumber triangles sandwiches off the petite paper doily and replaced it with the ring box.

When I said, "Amen," Rachel opened her eyes, saw the box, and started crying. Without even opening the jewelry box, she said she knew it was the ring she had been wanting for so long. That day, that tea party, that gift, scored very high on her chart of memorable moments.

If you've been saving a piece of special jewelry to pass on to your daughter, and/or if she highly values gifts, think of how you can incorporate a "bestowing moment" into your ongoing conversation with her. If she's too young to be responsible or to value an expensive piece of jewelry, you can still show it to her, tell her the story behind it, and promise that it will be hers one day. You'll keep it for her until she's a little older.

The objective is to do whatever makes her feel adorned and adored. When those messages of beauty and bestowing are communicated by a mom through gifts, it affirms to her daughter that she is of great value and highly cherished. To withhold such favor until she has "earned" the right carries a different message. Whether you intended it or not, you are communicating that she must always try hard to be good enough before she's rewarded.

Try to remember what you felt at her age. How important was it for you to receive gifts, words, hugs, attention, or kind services? What can you give to your daughter? Why not be extravagant about it?

The heart of a preadolescent girl is a treasure chest. She is busy collecting all that she deems important and keeps it locked in that treasure chest for safekeeping. The trouble with making hormone-induced decisions while she's out gathering gems is that not everything she holds on to is truly valuable. She holds on to what others say about her, how they treat her, and how they react when she enters a room or speaks up.

Do you see the potential power you hold? Your words, actions, and expressions must help to fill the vast openness of her heart. Her heart will gravitate to the voices that tell her she's important, smart, pretty or whatever quality she admires most in others and wants to attain.

> *Make sure your daughter receives*
> *her value statements at home*
> *so that she won't seek affirmation of her worth*
> *from hollow sources that will betray her.*

Let your voice be the first and the most convincing one to help her to feel loved and content. Help her to learn how to discern gold from fool's gold.

Other Options

Another way to mark the moment is to connect her coming-of-age-season with something that's of importance to her. Did you tell her she has to wait until she's older before she can get something special like take singing lessons? Has she been pleading to get her eyebrows shaped? At what age will she start shaving her legs? When is it time for her first bra?

Any of these pivotal moments can be turned into a small celebration. You bring the joy. You get to fancy-up the experience and help to take away the insecurity and embarrassment. With each small step forward, you are saying, "I'm here for you. I want to make fun memories with you."

Does your daughter save her birthday cards? Does she read carefully what family members write to her on those cards? This is the ideal chance for you to ask her grandmas, aunts, and close adult friends to send her cards that include encouragement and womanly advice. Let them know that, when the day comes for your special marking-the-moment celebration, you will deliver all the unopened missives to your daughter and remind her that these notes are from her women—her circle of ongoing support as she grows up.

If your daughter is shy and only comfortable when she's free to be her introverted self, why not share a journal or a book?

A Shared Journal

Start a written conversation between the two of you by sharing a journal. You can write a short paragraph or two on the first page, letting your daughter know that you love her. Invite her to write you back in the journal, and let her know this communication is just between the two of you. This is a safe place for her to ask questions, make comments, draw pictures—whatever she wants to share with you.

Make it a comfortable "just between us" experience. Put the journal under each other's pillow when you write something new so that it feels like you're exchanging secret notes. Write sweet things like, "I saw the way you helped your brother to tie his shoes today, and I loved the way you were so kind to him. You are an incredibly good sister."

As the communication becomes more comfortable, add specific subjects about how her body is changing. You might want to write, "I bought some new bodywash for you. It's in your shower. Let me know how you like it."

A day or two later, casually ask, "How did you like the new soap?" This might lead to a bit more explanation about how, as she's growing older, she'll be using new products to keep her body fresh. Baby steps. Small prep for what is to come.

A Book for Both of You

Are you and your daughter among the many moms and daughters who enjoy reading books together? It's a great way to have a shared experience as well as to use the book's content as a springboard for important conversations.

In my research to write *Preparing Your Daughter for Womanhood,* I read a lot of books that are written for pre-adolescent girls. While I liked parts of almost all of them, I didn't find one that I felt comfortable endorsing or listing as a resource in this book.

That said, I'd still encourage you to check out the many different books available for young girls and decide if one would work well for you. If you read it first, you will have a chance to take notes on specifics you would like to talk with your daughter about. You might want to write your thoughts in the margins or keep a list of key points.

That way, if you come to parts in the book that you aren't in complete agreement with, you can be prepared to go further than the book did or provide your daughter with more information or different information.

When you give the book to your daughter, make sure she knows that you want to talk about it with her. That could be through your shared journal, notes in the margins of the book, or a conversation.

Include Her

Busy lives mean that family members are orbiting in their own universes and rarely overlapping. Is that why "Bring Your Child to Work" Days and "Invite Your Parents to

School" Days were initiated? Did we need help to find ways to enter into each other's worlds? Maybe so.

How are things in your busy life these days? Can you think of a way you could easily include your daughter? Is there something you do that she often wants to hear about or be included in?

I have a Realtor friend who discovered that her daughter turned into an adorable hostess on open house days. No one could resist her smile when she pointed them to the plate of cookies on the counter next to the flyers and her mom's business card.

Another friend of mine who travels occasionally for her job made the effort to bring her daughter along to an event. Those three days became a turning point in their relationship.

One mom told me that her daughter seemed always to be underfoot when the mom was preparing dinner. She finally handed her daughter an apron, and the unplanned cooking lessons began. By the time the daughter was eleven, she eagerly prepared nearly all the family meals, and her favorite birthday gifts were cookbooks. By the age of twenty-four, she was an established chef, who by the way, had far surpassed her mom's cooking skills.

Try inviting your daughter to join you, when it makes sense, and use the experience to share your life with her as well as nurture the friendship part of your relationship.

Stories from Other Moms and Daughters

No Drop-Offs

When my daughter was nine, I read that as a mom I should never interfere with her journey of self-discovery by imposing anything on her because it would undoubtedly come with my own bias. The message was that my pre-adolescent daughter will become stronger and more independent if I only make informational material available and then step away so she can learn to develop her own problem-solving skills and thereby experience the empowering sense of self-sufficiency.

That made sense to me, so I bought a book about puberty and planned to leave it in my daughter's room. I told a friend what I was doing and she said, "When she was a baby and you knew she needed to be fed, did you ever once consider dropping a bottle in her crib and closing the door so she could develop her problem-solving skills and figure out how to feed herself?"

Our conversation became intense, but in the end, my friend helped me to realize that when my daughter was a baby, she needed me—my closeness, my voice, my expressions, my touch. She didn't need just the nourishment I put within her reach. At this next stage of her life, she needs all that, too. She needs more than a book on her nightstand.

I changed my plan and made dinner reservations for the

two of us. I'm a single mom so my daughter knew that getting dressed up and going to a nice restaurant twenty miles away was a big deal. I was nervous and afraid of how my daughter would react, but it went great.

During dinner I told her three things I liked about her, and I said that I knew God loved her and had His hand on her life. She cried. But then, she's been doing that a lot lately.

On the drive home she said she was embarrassed that she cried. I told her it was her hormones and that they are a good thing because they help a young girl's body change. She said she had been sneaking my deodorant and asked if she could get her own. We had a great conversation and stayed in the car to talk for almost an hour after we pulled into the parking structure at our apartment.

I told her about the book I had bought for her, and she asked if we could read it together. It went great, and we've had several important and helpful conversations since then. That night was a turning point in our relationship, and I'm so glad I made an effort to do something special, even though I was nervous and felt inadequate.

Oh, the Possibilities!

What are some ways that you might put the thoughts from this chapter into action? What portions of the chapter stood out to you?

Here's a list of possible points of action:

• Determine if your daughter responds best to words, gifts, or time together; think about how you can create a memorable moment of celebration.

• Get ready by purchasing or preparing a gift if you determine that's best for your girl.

• Buy a journal and take the first steps to use it in a conversational way between the two of you.

• Ask your daughter to pick a book for both of you to read together and discuss.

• Make plans to include your daughter in your busy life in a way that will (hopefully) be a positive time for both of you.

NOTES

Make Peace with Your Past

If you want to understand any woman
you must ask about her mother
and then listen carefully.

Anita Diamant, *The Red Tent*

Chapter Seven

Make Peace with Your Past

I t was important for me to add this chapter about your past because it all starts with you.

You know that, right?

You may have had an easy or at least easy-ish journey into adolescence. Your relationship with your mom may have been close then and is even closer now. You were nurtured well and so far, this book has provided you with some fun ideas on how you can keep the love and affection going into the next generation with your daughter.

If that's your story, what a gift you were given.

For other women, their past is more complicated. Their relationship with their mom wasn't ideal, and the hurts have stayed with them into this next season of life. If that's you, don't skip this chapter. It will help you to make peace with your past. I want you to be able to enter into these important conversations with your daughter with an uncluttered heart.

What do I mean by an uncluttered heart?

You know how renovation experts on TV shows can walk into a house and right away know what walls need to be removed to open the floor plan? They knock out old, load-bearing walls and install new, more efficient beams. They pull up stained carpets and know how to make the original wood floors come back to life. By the end of the show, the house is transformed into a spacious, breathing, light-filled, and inviting home.

Think of your heart in the same way. Do you have walls that need to come down? What's under that old carpet that you've tread upon for years? What windows need to be replaced?

Demo day! Put on your goggles and pick up your sledge-hammer. We need to get down to the framework by remembering your experience when your body changed. Go there with me.

Your Story

Start by answering these questions:

1. How old were you when you started your period?

2. Who was the first person you told?

3. What did you not understand about what your body was doing?

4. What questions did you have that you felt you were unable to ask?

5. What fears did you have about the change in your body?

If you and I were having this conversation over a nice cuppa English Breakfast tea, I can assure you that I'd be interested in hearing your answers. I've been listening to coming-of-age stories for many years, and at this point, I think I've heard it all. Nothing you would tell me would shock me.

Since we're not having this conversation face-to-face, is there someone you do feel comfortable talking with? Is there another mom, mentor, sister, or good friend who excels at listening and sharing? Start by asking each other the five questions above. You will find it can be surprisingly helpful to share your answers to these important life moments with a kindred spirit.

> ***It's so much friendlier with two.***
> A. A. Milne, *Winnie-the-Pooh*

Taking the time to contemplate your experience will do several things for you. First, it will increase your empathy for your daughter because, be honest, when was the last time you tried to remember how you felt when you were her age?

Second, the most important part of this exercise is to help you not to get stuck in the past but rather to focus on what is ahead with your daughter. You want to open the door to better possibilities in your future relationship with her.

Making peace with your past is a process. Healing is a process. Forgiveness is a process. When it comes to your past, give yourself space and grace. Stay open to the journey and keep taking those baby steps. Don't close off your heart.

A wise friend told me I should take time to do this sort of inventory of my journey into womanhood. She suggested this when my daughter was still a toddler because she said I needed to make sure I wasn't going to turn into a walking wounded mom who transferred my childhood hurts onto my daughter without realizing I was leaking toxic memories into her life.

At the time I struggled to respond to her advice, but she was right. It was important. Getting my heart uncluttered made a significant difference in both my life and my daughter's life. I had to do the hard work of looking over my shoulder, releasing the past hurts, and setting my heart and mind on what was ahead. That important process stripped away the anger and sense of humiliation I'd carried for years.

As a result, I'm able to tell the story of my entrance into puberty in an open and honest way without shrinking back in shame or getting tangled up in processing all those early adolescent emotions alongside the facts.

I'd like to share my journey with you now in hopes that it will help you to think through your experience. The sooner you can separate the truths from the lies and begin to heal from past hurts, the sooner you'll be free to start telling yourself your story in a liberating way. You'll be in a much healthier place mentally, spiritually, and emotionally as you enter into this next season of your daughter's life. Think of your healing as a gift she'll never know you gave her.

I Was Ten

My period started the second week of fifth grade when I was playing tetherball at recess. I forfeited my turn because

I felt like I had to go to the bathroom, but when I did, I couldn't figure out where the blood was coming from. I went through a lot of toilet paper and hoped it would go away.

On the second day, the cramping frightened me, and I thought that something was seriously wrong. Like, maybe I was dying! I finally went to my mom at the end of the day and told her I was bleeding.

"Get a Band-Aid," she said in her matter-of-fact way.

"I don't think we have any that are big enough."

"Why not?"

"Because. . ." I burst into tears and couldn't finish.

"What are you crying about?"

"It's coming from. . ." I pointed, still crying.

The look on my mom's face was complicated. I read it as partly surprise but mostly disgust. All she said was, "Don't you know what that is?"

I shook my head. I had no idea what was happening. No clues at all. None of my friends had matured as quickly as I had. No one I knew talked openly about such things.

"It's the curse," she mumbled. "Go to your room."

I was so confused. *The curse?* Had I done something wrong? The shame I felt was suffocating.

My flustered mother came in a few minutes later with a box of pads and a booklet. "Take this to the bathroom," she said. "Read it and take a shower before you use these."

I complied. An hour later I tried to act natural at the dinner table with my parents, my brother, and my sister. My mother didn't say anything. I would have been mortified if she had. Everything was "normal."

Except, it wasn't normal. Nothing felt natural. My body was doing strange things. I was sitting on a thick pad that felt odd and uncomfortable. My mind was still absorbing the clinical drawings of fallopian tubes and a uterus in the booklet that was held together by a single staple. I was so naïve. I never knew I was carrying around eggs. What in the world was sperm, and how did it get into a woman's uterus? I had so many questions. I felt overwhelmed and alone.

This was before the Internet so I couldn't privately Google my questions. Siri wasn't there to help me. I didn't know anyone I could ask; so I shut down inside.

My entrance into womanhood began with fear, shame, and isolation. What I learned that day was that growing up was something I had to figure out on my own. The pattern was set. I rarely went to my mom to tell her anything ever again.

During my high school years, I turned to friends, magazines, and books for information and advice. The unspoken message that had come through so clearly when I was ten and terrified was that if I ever went to my mother again with a problem, a question, or an issue, she would once again scowl at my immaturity and squelch discussion of any sort.

I knew I wanted my relationship with my children to be opposite of what I'd experienced. I wanted my daughter to feel that she could always come to me about anything.

Before that could happen, I had some internal work to do.

An Uncluttered Heart

For several decades I placed all the responsibility on my mother for our distant, seemingly uncaring relationship. If a singular person in this whole world should show their love and care for you by always being there for you, it should be your mother, right?

That was not the case for me. Something had to change before I could be the caring mom I wanted to be for my daughter. The first step was to make sure I didn't harbor unforgiveness toward my mom.

I don't know much about what my mom experienced during her childhood since she didn't talk about it. It wasn't possible for me to understand her struggles or pains or why her approach to many things came from a deep well of disapproval. She had a critical spirit. In my twenties, I was certain that I was nothing like her.

In my early thirties, during my second pregnancy, I heard myself lashing out at my mom with a bitter, cruel response when she pushed my buttons. It shocked me to realize I sounded just like her.

Now I was the one who had dug deep wells of resentment and filled them to the brim so that the poison was leaking out on those around me. I realized I was angry at her all the time. I didn't want to have any sort of relationship with her.

My husband said I turned into a different person when I was around her. I'd begun reverting to passive-aggressive tactics, like muttering negative comments under my breath or over-apologizing and acting as if it was a given fact that I couldn't do anything right. I withdrew and coddled my hurts.

Something had to change.

I remember the afternoon I poured out my heart to God. I asked Him to forgive me and to release me from my bitterness toward my mom. I remember saying aloud,

"No more!"

It was as if I'd drawn a line and told all the hurt from the past that it was no longer allowed to enter my present or my future. The dark-winged vulture of self-pity had to go fly. Shame was no longer given access to my heart. I asked God to remove all the resentment and hurt. I wanted Him to fling it back into the pit it came from. No more oppression. I wanted to be free to become the mom my children needed me to be.

As I prayed, I asked God to fill me with truth, the truth about His unfailing love for me and His extravagant grace. So much grace! I asked God to teach me how to extend that same abundant grace to myself, to my little family, and especially to my mom.

The healing process began immediately.

Notice, I said "process." Lots of ups and downs occurred as the years went on. But right away I felt as if I was released. I stopped expecting or even hoping to receive a nurturing level of communication from my mom. I accepted her where she was and knew that the choices now belonged to me. I could withhold kindness, affection, and loving care from her. Or I could give to her what she was either not willing or not able to give to me.

Grace and unconditional love became my superpowers in my newly renovated relationship with my mother. I wrote in my journal that I wanted to be "… remembered for what I do, not what was done to me."

Be gentle and ready to forgive; never hold grudges.
Remember, the Lord forgave you,
so you must forgive others.
Colossians 3:13, TLB

The more I chose to let go of the irritations and not return the jabs, the more empowered I became. Soon I was the one who directed our conversations and responded to her out of love. I stopped keeping a list of wrongs. I stopped envying relationships my friends had with their moms. Most importantly, I stopped expecting a different result.

What is that popular definition of insanity? "Doing the same thing over and over again but expecting a different result."

I stopped doing that. I got my sanity back, and I suddenly found a whole lot of open space in my uncluttered heart where God filled me with His love and His lavish gift of grace.

When He fills you up, there is more than enough love and grace to give to others. I've never run out of love for my mom. God's unconditional love. Best of all, I was free to enter my married and baby years with plenty of love and grace for my husband and children. I could be intentional about the family patterns that needed to change in this generation and focus on what needed to be established as a new foundation.

Start the Process

When you look over your shoulder and view your past, does it seem like too much to deal with? Does "uncluttering" sound simplistic? Maybe you're thinking that a major bulldozing would be a more realistic approach.

Okay. Fine. Go get a bulldozer.

Whatever it takes, move forward. Please! Don't get stuck. Don't put off your own healing. Take time to remove yourself from the rush of your life and dig deep into the lasting truth from God's Word. Schedule an appointment with a qualified counselor. Set up a heart-to-heart conversation with a mentor or close friend who will listen and pray for you. Whatever it takes, do it.

You know how to find resources. You know what you need. Take the steps to become healed, whole, and unhindered by anything in your past. You need to be free to focus on others and what they need rather than bogging down in past hurts. Self-pity is the worst. It can cripple you.

A big ah-ha moment for me came when I was watching *Sleepless in Seattle*. Rita Wilson was doing her great scene in which she's crying about the woman in the classic movie, *An Affair to Remember* and how Cary Grant came to see her at the end of the film. He didn't understand why she hadn't met him at the Empire State Building as planned. Why didn't she stand up, come to him, and embrace him? Instead, she stayed seated with a blanket over her legs. He had no idea she had been in a crippling accident.

I cried along with Rita because I realized that all these years I'd been emotionally standing there, confused, waiting for my mother to get up and come to me. And she simply couldn't.

Yet, I could go to her. I could choose to stay in the room, in the relationship. I could take her just as she was and choose to love her.

"I love you" were words I don't remember my mom using much while we were growing up. Maybe it's the rebel in me, but those are powerful words, and I decided to say them to her after my heart was uncluttered and I felt filled up with God's love and grace. I looked her in the eye and said, "I love you." She turned away and didn't respond.

I thought about her reaction for a while and decided it was okay. Even if she never echoed the truth back to me, I found I was free to say those words to her, from my heart, whenever I felt compelled to do so. And I did.

I'll never forget the phone call when I was in my early fifties, and I ended it with the same, "I love you, Mom," that I'd been saying to her out of sincerity for almost a decade. That day, she returned them. "I love you, too."

It makes my heart happy to tell you that I've heard my mom tell me many times that she loves me. Not at the beginning of my days. The words came at the end of her days. The truth and power of sincere love covered a multitude of hurts and led us into the process both of us went through as we experienced God's healing. Each time she said it, I received it.

Put on Your Oxygen Mask First

When you deal with your issues and needs first, you can then give your daughter what she needs. You might even be able to give your mom something she always has needed. Doing the important work of your own self-care first is a lot like the safety instructions repeated on every flight before taking off: "Place your oxygen mask over your nose and mouth first before assisting your child."

The airlines even give us visuals for this important step, not only in preflight videos but also in demonstrations by flight attendants who show us how it's done in case of an emergency.

In some ways, we are all in a state of emergency in our culture and in our families today. So many influences would like nothing more than to hijack our relationships with our daughters and take control, or worse, take us both down in flames. The rules of preparedness apply. You take care of yourself first. Then give your daughter what she needs.

The greatest truth in all this is that God can do anything. He can set you free in the unseen realm where chains of shame, guilt, anger, unforgiveness, and resentment may have linked the women in your family for generations.

Please. Be the one who draws the line and says, "No more." Reach for your oxygen mask.

A new story will begin in you, for you, through you. This new pattern will define not only your daughter's passage into womanhood. But also—think of this—your release and freedom can potentially affect all the women in your future lineage. Women who are yet to be born will be affected by the choices you make in this generation. Pretty astounding, isn't it?

If you're not sure where to start with all the internal spring cleaning, start with this prayer.

Create in me a clean heart,
O God, and put a new and right spirit within me.
Psalm 51:10, NRSV

Stories from Other Moms and Daughters

Speaking the Truth in Love

My mom always made a big deal about everything. She loved putting on celebrations. I'm a private person and never liked her grand parties. I learned when I was young that if I told her anything personal, she would tell everyone. It's how her big family did things. I'm more like my dad, quiet and shy. He loves my mom and her vivacious personality. I always saw them as an opposites-attract sort of couple. But growing up, I never felt secure around my mom.

I was eleven when I started my period. I knew plenty because everything was discussed openly in our house. What terrified me was the thought of what my mom might say or do when I told her. So, I didn't. I was so frightened I remained silent for months and months and found ways to take care of everything I needed without her knowing.

I felt so guilty. When I was twelve, I wrote her a letter saying that I kept it a secret because I couldn't deal with the attention that I knew she would want to place on me. I remember thinking I was so mature because in my letter I told her I had trust issues.

She was hurt, and for the next decade, we pretty much kept our distance from each other. I know it was painful for both of us, but I didn't know how to make an inroad to try to change the patterns that had been set.

When I was twenty-one, I started seeing a female Christian counselor. Those sessions were a turning point in my life. I wrote my mom another letter at the end of my last counseling session. This time I thanked her for all the ways she had loved me and been a caring mom, and I invited her to meet me for lunch. I couldn't believe how much we cleared up during those two hours. For the first time I felt like she accepted me just the way I am, as an introvert. I think I began to understand and accept her, too.

When I turned twenty-five, she wanted to throw a big party, and believe it or not, I told her I would like that. It was the best party. It really was. She loved it, and so did I. I felt like I had entered a new season with her, and all the anxiety from my timid preteen years was no longer an issue.

I'm grateful for our renovated relationship. I don't know what my life would be like if I didn't have my mom in it the way she is now. I learned that it's never too late to try to connect with your mom.

Oh, the Possibilities!

What are some ways that you might put the thoughts from this chapter into action? What portions of the chapter stood out to you?

Here's a list of possible points of action:

• Take time to evaluate where you are in your relationship with your mom.

• Do what you need to do to settle the unresolved issues from your childhood.

• Talk to someone who understands and can help you to make peace with your past.

• Spend time praying, releasing, forgiving those who treated you unfairly.

• Don't return to unhealthy thought-ruts that you've tromped through over the years.

• Create new thought patterns and do your part in restoring broken relationships.

• Strap on your oxygen mask first before helping your daughter.

NOTES

Focus on the Future

Now glory be to God,
who by his mighty power at work within us
is able to do far more than we would ever dare to ask
or even dream of—
infinitely beyond our highest prayers,
desires, thoughts, or hopes.

Ephesians 3:20, TLB

Chapter Eight

Focus on the Future

Our Heavenly Father has been with you from the beginning of your existence and the beginning of your daughter's existence. When you step back and take in the big picture, you'll see that He is already at work in this season of your life and your daughter's life. He is able to do more than you could ever imagine. More than you could ever dream.

This is the truth that fills all of us moms with hope.

By taking the time to read this book and think about what's best for your daughter, you already are focusing on the future. You are pouring all kinds of goodness, grace, truth, and love into the next generation.

Once again, I applaud you. Well done.

Now what about that small matter of sharing the details of your past and your experiences with your girl? What does she need to know about your childhood? What will help and what might hurt?

This is the best time for you to think about what you want to share and how to do it in a way that will enrich your daughter's life.

Think of all the good times in your childhood. Remember the sweet memories and let those good things be the opening lines of your conversation. Pour out all the happy stories and the sweet memories. Don't hold back. Share the simple joys that shaped you during your early years.

**Repeat all the kind things that were
done to you and for you.
Give out of the abundance that was given to you.**

When your thoughts come to rest on childhood hurts, and you know that one day you'll want to share deeper, more complex memories with your daughter, I hope you'll spend some time going over this chapter. Think through what really matters in the big picture.

The following three questions are the ones I've been asked the most often. I hope the replies will help to give you some encouraging insights. I know you want to make wise choices with your words. You want to turn the focus onto what is to come and not get stuck on what came before.

1. How much should I tell my daughter about my experience as a young girl?

Start slowly, please. She doesn't need to know everything about your life when she's seven. She really doesn't. And she especially doesn't need to feel as if everything that happens in her life is placed next to the yardstick of your life and measured by your experiences. Who among us likes to hear statements that begin with, "When I was your age..."?

If your growing-up years include significant events you've had to process in-depth, measure out those details little by little. Only share what's needed. Guard her innocence.

A friend of mine answered her seven-year-old daughter's question about who someone was in an old family photo by saying, "That's your grandpa's brother."

She was prepared to add, "He was mean to my sister and me when we were little. He did things to us he shouldn't have. It was really sad."

However, she caught herself and realized that nothing more needed to be said. She could give her daughter more details when she grew older if it would genuinely benefit her daughter to hear her whole story. This wasn't the time to tell her little girl about the childhood abuse and court trial that divided the family and sent her uncle to prison for four years.

What mattered was that, as a mom, she knew how to be on the alert to protect her daughter and to train her daughter how to protect herself. The reasons she was so in tune with those instincts didn't need to be the starting point of that ongoing and growing conversation.

Think of the way you share the truth with your daughter in terms of how much salt is needed to make a cookie recipe turn out delicious. You only need ¼ teaspoon, not 2 cups. Just a sprinkle. Salt may be part of the recipe, but it's not the key ingredient. Your past experiences are part of your relationship with your daughter, but they aren't the main ingredient.

During her preadolescent years, you're creating a recipe for how your communication will continue and grow in the years to come. If you've produced a bad batch, so to speak, due to going heavy on the salt and forgetting to add any sugar, it's okay. Start over. Pay attention to your measurements this time. Keep trying until your recipe for communication has just the right amounts.

What should the key ingredient be? I believe it should be grace. Big scoops of grace for you and heaping cupsful of grace for your daughter.

You know how some recipes read, "in a separate bowl" or "divide the yolks from the egg whites"? The same step-by-step process of separating might be part of your personal family recipe. Grace allows for you to separate your relationship with your mom from your daughter's relationship with her. It allows you to process and heal from past violations in your own bowl while mixing a different part of your daughter's life recipe in another bowl.

Remember that you're putting your oxygen mask on first. You're uncluttering your heart and not forcing her to go through the process with you. Think about the analogy of how all the broken pieces of your life can be soldered together into stained glass so that when the light shines through, it tells a beautiful story.

You have a lot going on in your own season of life. All of it will eventually be sifted and mixed into her life. For now, though, please don't dump everything on her at once.

Like many families, we have a few people in our clan who have demonstrated by their life choices that they would not be a safe person for our kids to spend time with. In those cases, we provided uncomplicated explanations about why we stepped away or limited our time with them. We wanted our children to learn how to be discerning and, at the same time, confident that we wouldn't throw them into a situation where it was up to them to protect themselves.

As my daughter grew older, she tuned in to some of the ways my mom would disapprove of things I said or did. That's when she felt her own tug-of-war with her grandma and made self-protecting adjustments along the way. As Rachel shared with me her feelings about her grandma, I shared more of my feelings and pieces of my experiences with my mom.

By that time, I'd healed a lot and wasn't trying to get my daughter on my side or use her as a therapist. It really is possible to speak the truth in love when you've done the important work of uncluttering your heart.

> ***Instead, we will speak the truth in love,***
> ***growing in every way more and more like Christ. . .***
> Ephesians 4:15, NLT

As you work on your communication recipe with your daughter regarding your past experiences, please remember that most emotionally fluctuating preteens haven't developed a balanced sense of understanding and discernment. The maturity will come. Be patient.

If I had unloaded all my experiences, opinions, and feelings on Rachel when she was still a girl, she would have been overloaded and would have missed out on experiencing her own important moments with her grandma, other relatives, and family friends. It was my responsibility to separate my feelings and let her develop her own relationships.

2. How do I know what to say to my daughter?

The quick answer is to pray for wisdom, as James 1:5a (NLT) encourages us to do.

> ***If you need wisdom, ask our generous God,***
> ***and he will give it to you.***

That's the best first step for a parent in any situation, no matter how old your children are. Whenever possible, give yourself enough space to think through and pray about what needs to be said and how and when you should initiate the topic. Ask God to show you what to say, how to say it, and especially when to say it.

A friend of mine had a complicated journey through her teen years. She planned to share openly with her daughter about how she became pregnant at fifteen and the fear-driven choice she made in isolation to end the pregnancy. Over the years she had made peace with her past and knew that God had redeemed her and brought good from that painful time in her life.

Unfortunately, instead of having the freedom to share her story with her daughter at the time and in the way she wanted to talk about it, a relative chose to enlighten her nine-year-old daughter. Her daughter came to her in tears, saying, "Why did you kill our baby?"

My friend stopped everything and sat down with her. This is how she described that difficult conversation.

"I started by telling her that my childhood was quite different from hers. I didn't have anyone I could talk to, and I didn't understand how my body worked or how overwhelming my emotions could be. I told her I kept making poor choices that led to more bad choices and I was very sorry for those decisions, but I knew God forgave me when I asked Him to.

"It was a really difficult conversation, and all the way through I kept asking God to give me wisdom. The thought that kept coming to me was that I needed to have discretion. I knew I could give her more details later if I needed to. But in that intense moment I only needed to say enough to let my daughter know that she could always come to me to talk about difficult things and be assured that I would tell her the truth."

Since that first painful conversation, my friend and her daughter have had half a dozen more comfortable talks about sexual intimacy, peer pressure, fear-based choices, and the sanctity of life. Even though the topic started in an unwelcomed way, she's grateful for the closeness it created between them. Her daughter is now fifteen and experiencing a different adolescence than my friend did because of the big-picture discussions that helped her to understand how to make good choices.

3. Things are different now than when I was her age. She knows so much more than I did. Why shouldn't I get everything out into the open?

It's true, and kind of sad that culture and communication have changed so dramatically since you were ten years old. One thing hasn't changed. The elegance of discretion.

Have you heard the term, "A word fitly spoken . . ."? It comes from Proverbs 25:11a. I like how *The Message* expresses the thought.

Isn't that a good image? Choosing the best thing to say at the right time is as considerate as giving a beautiful gift that was made especially for that person.

The right word at the right time is like a custom-made piece of jewelry.

I learned how beautiful discretion can be when I spent time with a woman named Ethel. She was older than I, and in due time, she became my writing mentor. She was a published author when we first met, and I was still trying to get my first article published. I hadn't even started to write a book yet, but I blithely approached her with a long list of questions about what it was like to be a writer and what I needed to do to get published.

She answered very few of my questions with specific details. Instead, Ethel graciously invited me to join a writer's critique group that she hosted at her home. For six years we met once a month and little by little she taught me the essentials of the writing craft. As our friendship grew, I realized how bold my starry-eyed novice self had been when I first approached her. She measured out the realities of writing for publication step-by-step, with discretion.

Our friendship continued for several decades, and she became a sheltering tree for me. The rain came, but because of her closeness, I wasn't doused all at once. We confided in each other, and she shared about the losses, injustices, and disappointments she experienced in the publishing world. Every setback or failure that I experienced I knew I could share with her because she understood.

I look back now and see that if she had given me all her insights, experiences, and gut-level truths at one time, I would have been overwhelmed. I might have become so discouraged I would have given up before finishing my first novel.

But I wasn't overwhelmed or jaded by the process because she exercised the beautiful gift of discretion. I didn't need to know everything at once. I didn't need to carry with me the disappointments and rejections she had experienced on her journey. I could go at my own pace, knowing that she walked beside me and would answer each question with just the right amount of information and elegant discretion.

She gave me the tools I needed so that I could make the next choice about what I should do with all the options in front of me as a writer.

As you mentor your daughter, always consider how you might guard her heart. You are her sheltering tree. Give her the tools she needs to make good choices.

Discretion isn't a common topic, is it? It's more likely that you've heard the popular thought that we have the right to openly talk about everything that happens to us, and if people didn't want us to tell about their bad behavior, they should have treated us differently.

As true as that is, I would like to add this thought. As a woman of options, I have the freedom and right to tell all. *And* I also have the freedom to choose discretion. The right word at the right time.

I think of discretion as the *Selah* of relationships. You

know how the word "Selah" appears in the Psalms after truth has been declared? The common interpretation is that listeners and worshippers were being directed to pause. To reflect. To consider what they had just heard before responding. It's a discretionary sort of action.

There's a time and place for the whole story to be told. And it should be. As a woman of options, I hope you'll be discerning about what you share with your daughter and when. Blend truth with grace. Pause and have a Selah moment where you reflect and consider before going on.

Stories from Other Moms and Daughters

It's Not Too Late

When my daughter was fifteen, I heard you talk about doing something special with our daughters before they start their period. I wish I had heard your talk about five years earlier because I know it would have meant a lot to her if I had done something.

But I decided it wasn't too late, so I thought through all my options based on what means the most to her, and I knew she'd like it if I went to coffee with her. We started going on Friday afternoons at four o'clock.

The first time we went, I pulled out a magazine and said I was thinking of getting my hair cut like the woman in the picture. I asked what she thought. She pulled up pictures on her phone and showed me other styles she thought would look better. One of them I really liked so I asked her to send it to me so I could show the hair stylist.

She ended up going with me to the appointment because the earliest opening was for the next Friday at four. We bought coffee first, and she sipped her latte while I got a haircut. I liked how it turned out, and she told everyone it was her suggestion.

The next Friday I read to her a page from a novel I was reading that was set in Italy because I liked the vivid description and wanted to share it with her. The next week she brought a project she had been working on in her art class and opened her usually hidden sketchbook so I could see her work.

We have kept this tradition going almost every Friday for the past few years. I know it probably sounds strange that we live in the same house but have to schedule a coffee date to get to know each other better. But it's working. We share little bits of our lives and talk about all kinds of things because it's just the two of us.

On her birthday, when she turned eighteen, I gave her my present during our Friday coffee date. It was a coupon I made for a weekend trip to Seattle and dinner in the Space Needle. I knew that was something she had wanted to do for a long time. Inside the card I had written that I loved her and was proud of her. Then I wrote, "You are an exceptional woman. I have loved being by your side for your journey into your adult years. I hope you know I will always be here for you." We both cried. That was our moment. Eye-to-eye, heart-to-heart.

I often think that she was at a crossroads when she was fifteen, but we hardly talked about anything personal during the rush of every day. If you hadn't challenged us as moms to do something special with our daughters, I don't want to think about all that I would have missed out on!

I told my friend what I was doing with my daughter and that prompted her to take horseback riding lessons with her sixteen-year-old. On a trail ride in the woods last year, her daughter told her she had been waiting and hoping for the day when her mother would start being her friend as well as her mom. The change in their relationship is amazing.

You're right. As moms, we need to take the first step, and we should never think it's too late.

Oh, the Possibilities!

What are some ways that you might put the thoughts from this chapter into action? What portions of the chapter stood out to you?

Here's a list of possible points of action:

• Thank God for His mighty power at work in you. Believe that He is able to do far more than you would ever dare to ask or even dream.

• Think of the good things that were woven throughout your childhood and become intentional about telling those stories and speaking well of the people who loved you and were kind to you.

• Ask God to give you wisdom to know what to say to your daughter about your past and when to say it.

• Think about how to incorporate discretion in your conversations with your daughter.

• Find ways to connect more with your daughter and to start building more bridges.

• Give yourself the freedom and grace to start over or to start now to become a sheltering tree and affirming voice in your daughter's life.

NOTES

Bring the Sacred

*If you extract the precious from the worthless,
you will become My spokesman.*

Jeremiah 15:19b, NASB

Chapter Nine

Bring the Sacred

This might be my favorite chapter in *Preparing Your Daughter for Womanhood* because I love seeing the eternal brought into the commonness of life. It enlivens me to spend time thinking and studying concepts that are eternal and then expressing them in ways that are easy to understand.

I've always liked the imagery in this William Blake poem written more than two hundred years ago:

> **To see a World in a Grain of Sand**
> **And a Heaven in a Wild Flower**
> **Hold Infinity in the palm of your hand**
> **And Eternity in an hour...**

We are surrounded by the beauty and holiness of the One

who created us. What a gift we have to give our daughters in helping them to see the wonders of God's goodness in the midst of all the horrible things that happen in this world.

What Can I Bring?

A few years ago, some of us women at our church put our heads together to plan a bridal shower for one of our dearly loved college girls. My friends each named what she was going to bring—decorations, dessert, etc. We were at the end of the list, and I hadn't jumped in yet.

"What can I bring?" I asked.

"You bring the sacred," the hostess said. "That's what you do best."

I remember feeling my heart flutter with the anticipation that I would do something at this shower that would elevate it beyond a time of gifts, food, and games. We were gathering to celebrate a sacred event. Two would soon become one in holy matrimony, and as her women, we were launching the young bride into the next season of her life.

I brought a special devotional thought inspired by Bible verses that seemed applicable specifically to the bride-to-be. I teared up a bit, and so did she, as I blessed her. The moment felt like candlelight to me in that circle of women. Flickering, warming, and touching all of us in that circle. I love bringing the sacred.

Some of my friends would be a wreck if they were told they had to come up with something meaningful to say in a moment like that. They, however, are the ones who have other gifts, the ones I do not possess. They show up with mouthwatering appetizers arranged to perfection on heirloom platters.

They find the perfect gift and wrap it so beautifully that the guest of honor says she doesn't want to unwrap it and spoil it. They are the ones who are willing to step out of the circle of smiles and stories to stand in the corner where they listen quietly as one of the other guests pours out her heart. A vibrant sacredness exists in all their offerings.

Here's my challenge to you, willing moms. Ask yourself, what is your gift that you bring to your daughter as well as to other women in your circle? Tap into what you're gifted at and explore that fully as you walk side-by-side with your daughter over the bridge into womanhood. Don't try to be who you're not.

Your daughter will recognize right away if you attempt to arrange something that's supposed to be meaningful but none of it rings true to who you are or where you feel most at home.

If you would never feel comfortable with a teacup in your hand, then don't even consider a tea party. If the great outdoors is where you feel at home, then take her outside for your heart-to-heart conversation. Let her see the delight on your face and feel the sense of worship happening naturally when you gaze up at the sky or reach for an amber leaf on a crisp fall day and twirl it between your fingers.

Yes, you want to understand her love language and consider what's most comfortable for her, as I've mentioned in earlier chapters. That's where you want to start because it shows you're making the effort to help her to feel at ease, especially if you have an inkling that the first conversation or two will be uncomfortable for her.

Then, as your friendship grows and the conversation continues, invite her into where and how you feel closest to God.

Let her share the intimacy of watching you be your truest self.

If music is your sweet spot, expand the ways you share that personal passion with her. Do you feel closest to God when you're in church? Invite her to sit beside you and be surrounded by all the elements of the service. She might not yet have found the most natural way that she connects with God. Introduce her to more than what she's known in her childhood traditional exercises in faith. Include her in broader, more grown-up expressions of worship.

Doing Your Job

A few days ago a friend who has a preteen daughter told me that she felt as if she had been "cut adrift" and was no longer included in what she considered to be the most important mentoring part of her daughter's life.

"What happened?" I asked.

"I knew she was upset about something, so I did what I always have tried to do. I asked her if she wanted to talk about whatever was bothering her."

"Did she close down?" I suggested.

My friend nodded, looking so forlorn.

In a weak attempt to offer comfort, I said, "It's typical at that age, you know."

"I know. But it wasn't as if she was pulling back, sulking, or stomping off to her room."

"What did she do?"

My friend sighed. "She looked at me with the sweetest expression and said she wanted to go talk to God about everything first and then she would tell me after she had poured out her heart to Him first."

"That's beautiful," I said.

"I know. It's beautiful and mature, and I'm a horrible person because I feel like I'm jealous of God right now."

We laughed softly, the way close friends do.

"You're not a horrible person," I told her. "You are a mom who did a great job of showing your daughter how to go to God with everything, and now that's what she's doing on her own."

"I just wish she wasn't such a fast learner."

We smiled and talked about how quickly children grow and how much they pick up from us. My friend had brought the sacred into her daughter's life, and for all the years ahead, her daughter would know how to keep developing that closeness to God. He would always be there for her and with her no matter where she went or what happened in her life.

The Story of the Fine China Plate

If you're not sure where to start or how to incorporate a sense of the sacred as your daughter advances on her journey to womanhood, maybe this true story will help. The imagery blossomed from a real-life moment I experienced with the daughter of my closest friend. It became an often-repeated analogy of how to explain the concept of holiness and sanctification to a child.

Years ago, when my kids were toddlers, they were napping on a summer afternoon while I was in the backyard picking cherries from our tree. I'd filled a bowl and was taking them inside to wash them when my friend dropped off her nine-year-old daughter, Natalie, and asked if she could stay for a few hours.

Natalie was quiet as she watched me pat the cherries dry and dip them in a saucepan of warm chocolate. As I lined up the chocolate cherry treats on waxed paper, I asked if something was bothering her.

"It's just not fair," she said. "All my friends went to the movies, but my parents said I couldn't go. They said it wasn't the kind of movie I should see."

She sighed. "My parents are too protective of me. They said they wanted me to stay clean. What does that even mean?"

I knew she was eyeing the cherries, and I wanted to share some with her, but I wanted to make it special. Her question sparked an idea.

"Would you like some cherries?"

"Yes, I would."

I went to the kitchen garbage and pulled out a dirty paper plate stained with beans and hot dogs from last night's barbecue.

"You're not going to use that dirty plate, are you?" she asked.

I shrugged, holding the paper plate in my hand, waiting.

"Don't you have any other plates to use?"

"Oh, yes." I returned the paper plate to the garbage and went over to the antique hutch. "I have other plates. They're special plates. Clean plates. Plates that I have kept set apart."

Natalie watched as I opened the door and lifted out a single, fine china plate. "I'm probably overly protective of these plates," I told her. "They're valuable and beautiful. They were a gift to me, and I treasure them so I want to always keep them clean and ready so I can use them to serve others."

A flicker of understanding shone in Natalie's eyes. "It's a

beautiful plate," she said as I placed it in front of her with the yummy chocolate-covered cherries.

"Yes, it is," I agreed. "And so are you, Natalie. You are more valuable than you can even imagine. God gave you to your parents as a special gift. Don't you see? You've been set apart, too."

"That's why they're so protective of me," she said in a low voice. "I'm not a paper plate to them."

"No, you're not. You are a fine china plate, and you've been set apart so that your heart will stay clean, and you'll be ready to serve others with honor and beauty."

Natalie tilted her head. "Did my mom tell you to say all this?"

"No."

"Then where did this come from?"

I smiled because the concept of being set apart wasn't mine, and it wasn't new. It was ancient and had been expressed many times by God in His Word.

"It came from the same place all the best truth comes from. The Bible."

Natalie looked surprised. "I didn't know the Bible said anything about plates."

I went into the other room and came back with my Bible. "It's right here. Listen. 'If you stay away from sin you will be like one of these dishes made of purest gold—the very best in the house—so that Christ himself can use you for his highest purposes.'"

I showed her the verse in 2 Timothy 2:21 in *The Living Bible*.

You will be like one of these dishes made of purest gold.

"Your parents are helping you to stay clean in your heart and in your mind by keeping you set apart from things in this world that they believe aren't good for you."

Later that afternoon, when Natalie was ready to go home, I had a gift for her. I'd written 2 Timothy 2:21 on the back of one of my treasured fine china plates, and I handed it to her with a big smile. "You are a fine china plate," I told her. "Never forget that."

Natalie hung the plate in a prominent spot on her bedroom wall. As her body, mind, heart, and soul sauntered into her teen years, the china plate was a gentle reminder that she was greatly treasured and set apart to stay clean so that Christ could use her for His noble purposes. Many of the choices she made in those years and beyond were influenced by that simple conversation we had that summer afternoon.

The impression was made because the moment was holy. The conversation focused on God's truth. On His values. On what matters for eternity.

You and I have no idea what can happen when we bring the sacred. I hope we never miss the opportunity to elevate those rare and wonderful moments when God's Spirit inspires us to share truth, hope, and light with our daughters. I hope you'll find joy in bringing a little more to birthdays, holidays, and one-to-one conversations by looking for the eternal and finding your best way to express it.

Initiate a Deeper Conversation

Here are three ways you can turn your thoughts to a more worshipful approach in your ongoing conversation with your daughter:

1. Tell her she was wanted

Were you elated when you found out you were pregnant? Then tell her that. Let her see your smile when you say how you couldn't wait to get your first ultrasound and hear her heartbeat. Describe how it felt the first time you felt her fluttering inside and how you sang to her and prayed for her or whatever it was that began between the two of you before you even saw each other face-to-face. Tell her how you loved her before she was born.

Share with your daughter how in awe you were when she was born. Or when you first met her. Or how you felt when you started the adoption process and hoped that God would bring her into your life. Talk about how God worked in your life to bring her to life. Tell her she was wanted then, and she is wanted now.

What you say and the way you say it doesn't have to be unrealistically mushy or as romantic as I might be making it sound. Just say what's true, from your heart.

2. Demonstrate the sacred

Develop a pattern of praying with her regularly. If praying aloud is still something you're developing in your life, be willing to learn alongside her. Start with simple, honest words. Thank God for what He's given you and done for you. Invite her to add whatever she wants to your prayer.

Blessing your children each night is a wonderful pattern to develop. We did this when our kids were young and continued it when they were teens. I still remember those nights when they would head upstairs to bed and call out, "Are you going to come and bless me?" We always answered yes.

It's a privilege to be the one who gets to bless her at the end of her day. You are the one who is speaking the name of our Heavenly Father over her in a sacred way. Think of how many times a day she might hear God's name spoken in an unsacred way. You are showing that God is holy.

Consider this. If you don't demonstrate to her how to pray and express a sense of reverence in communicating with God, who will? From what other sources is she discovering what it looks like to have an intimate relationship with her Heavenly Father?

3. Worship openly

For many, worship is a personal experience. When you are open and share that part of yourself with your daughter, your vulnerability in expressing your spiritual self will invite her to express her soul-level feelings with you. Shared worship is an added and much needed closeness that will carry the two of you through difficult times in the years ahead. You're teaching her that the inner life is of high value. The connection to the eternal and the freedom to express her heart are essential dimensions of her life.

It has been my life rhythm to read my Bible and pray and journal during the week. When our children were young, I always sat in my favorite snuggle chair for these quiet times of worship. On the end table next to the chair, I'd light a candle. My kids knew that if they saw me in that chair, with my Bible open or my head bowed and the candle lit, they were to leave me alone and not interrupt. I was in an important meeting with the King of the Universe, and I was probably talking to Him about them! They saw what worship looked like for their mom and learned to respect those sacred moments.

Stories from Other Moms and Daughters

God Was Always There

My mom didn't grow up going to church and didn't have much Christian influence in her younger years. When I was eight, she and my dad gave their lives to Christ and wanted to raise their children differently than they had been.

I think my mom did a good job of figuring out what was important, based on what she wished she had been told or given. She bought matching Bibles for us, and we started a game of trying to find different verses. We would both underline them, and when we went to church and wrote notes in the margins, we would compare what we had learned. It was all new to both of us at the same time so that made the discoveries fun.

When I was eleven, our family was sitting around the firepit in our backyard on a summer night. The topic of sex and puberty somehow came up, and my parents talked to my brother and me in a relaxed and open way. That's where I learned everything I needed to know at that age. I didn't feel uncomfortable then, but when I started my period a few months later, I felt really embarrassed and didn't want anyone except my mom to know.

My mom set up a special day for just the two of us and told me it was a Celebration of Menstruation, which sounded so strange to me, but at the same time, it made what had happened to my body feel more normal. We went shopping and out to lunch. Throughout the day she said a lot of positive things about how proud she was of me and how she could see God's love in my life.

What I remember most was that when we got home, she reached over and took my hand. She told me I was pretty, smart, and kind. Then she prayed and thanked God for making me and letting her be my mom. It was a lot sweeter than I'm making it sound.

It's one of my favorite memories because not only did I feel grownup and included in the world of womanhood, but I felt like she showed me how God's presence is over everything in life. It was like the natural way she and my dad had talked about sex around the firepit. I knew then that I always wanted to be aware of God's presence. I knew that He was always there, and I wanted to grow closer to Him, the way my mom and I were growing closer.

Oh, the Possibilities!

What are some ways that you might put the thoughts from this chapter into action? What portions of the chapter stood out to you?

Here's a list of possible points of action:

• Think about the things that you do well and that bring you joy. How do you see them as a way of sharing what is sacred or using them in an act of worship?

• Where have you held back in letting your daughter learn from how you communicate with God and how you are growing in your relationship with Him?

• What can you do that would open wider channels between your daughter and you in your spiritual lives?

• What is one simple way that you can express to your daughter today that God is with her and that He loves her?

NOTES

Women Like Us

The world is a book,
and those who do not travel
read only a page.

St. Augustine

Chapter Ten

Women Like Us

Have you noticed how much your view of life changes when you realize that other people in other parts of the globe are having the same experiences as you are? We're not isolated as moms, as women. Every woman in the world from the beginning of time has been part of the experience of menstruation.

When I was fourteen, our family took a trip around the U.S. in a camper. The three of us kids groaned every time we stopped at another Civil War battlefield site or parked overnight in the driveway of the home of another relative we had never met before. But by the end of the long journey, something unexpected had happened.

Our young views and understanding of other people, places, and cultures had expanded.

This happened naturally as we were introduced to such

things as a Hopi ceremonial dance in Arizona and a tour of Williamsburg where guides in period costumes demonstrated what life was like during the American Revolution.

We connected with so many interesting people. One sultry night in Tennessee, I chased fireflies with a girl I had just met named Judy. In Texas we swung on a rope over a swimming hole with local kids who owned their own horses. We made s'mores with our campground neighbors while in North Carolina. We paddled a canoe on one of Minnesota's one thousand lakes and listened to our uncle recite Longfellow's epic poem, "Hiawatha."

Our family connections became vivid, and relatives became familiar. The United States became a living, breathing country, alive with stories, accents, tastes, and sights that I never would have understood growing up in Southern California's beach culture.

Cultures and Common Ground

In a similar way, as I was researching and compiling content for this book, my appreciation for women in other places and cultures expanded. It became a virtual tour through history and around the world, listening to how coming-of-age has been viewed and celebrated in various cultures over the centuries.

I discovered many references to rituals, chants, and instructions on how a young girl can awaken her inner goddess. Menstruation was observed in a ritualistic way with red foods that aligned the child-turned-woman with the moon, the tides, and her Zodiac sign. Prayers to Mother Earth were included.

Those entrance-to-womanhood incantations made me wish more writers were crafting books like this one. I believe women are empowered and aligned when they look beyond the elements of this physical sphere and humbly bow before the One who created them and created the whole universe. All power and life come from Father God, the One who made heaven and Earth.

This is what our daughters need to hear from us many times over because other voices will always be in the background. When our daughters understand that God made their intricate bodies and when they believe that He is the Giver of life and health and all that makes us distinctly female, their inner strength will grow and be anchored in truth.

> ***Thank you for making me so wonderfully complex!***
> ***It is amazing to think about. Your workmanship***
> ***is marvelous—and how well I know it.***
> Psalm 139:14 TLB

As you read the following highlighted global traditions, you might see a connection to your family heritage. The knowledge of where the women of your family have come from will undoubtedly give you a sense of understanding for your mother and grandmother. Not all traditions are included, but you'll see that many of them come from a sacred foundation.

A Global Overview

Jewish Customs

The first recorded account of Bar Mitzvahs for boys was in France during the Middle Ages. No specific coming-of-age ceremony is referred to in the Old Testament. Details about Bat Mitzvahs for girls can be traced back to the late nineteenth century. It was to be a day of happiness when a daughter would enter the obligation of the commandments. This occurs when she is twelve or thirteen, depending on whether the family is Orthodox, Conservative, or Reformed.

Bat Mitzvahs gradually grew into more lavish affairs that included blessings, feasting, dancing, and a toast by the parents. Usually the father offers thanks to God that he is no longer held responsible for his child's sins. The gathering of family and friends at the event demonstrates the support the young girl can rely on and is symbolic of how she is now to establish her place in her Jewish community.

High Church Customs

In Catholic, Anglican, Orthodox, and other high churches, both boys and girls are "confirmed" after they have taken their first Communion. The confirmation ceremony comes at a child's "age of accountability," which generally is between eight and twelve years old. Before confirmation, children are prepared to understand and receive their first Communion at a service attended by family and friends.

In some churches girls traditionally don beautiful white dresses to represent their purity and are crowned with a wreath of flowers. In some countries such as Spain, Germany, Luxembourg, and Austria, young girls are dressed as brides. Boys wear suits in most countries, but in Scotland they wear kilts. In Switzerland both boys and girls wear simple white robes with a wooden crosses around their necks.

India

In many parts of India and other countries that observe Hinduism, when a girl has her menarche, she has attained the ability to bear children, and her newly blossomed sexuality is celebrated by a grand party called *Ruthu Sadangu* or *Pen Vaisu Vanthachu*. Some communities maintain that the coming-of-age rites must be performed on the day the girl starts her period.

Purifying rituals are performed by women in the extended family, and a time of isolation for the girl is included. This is followed by a large party with gifts and rich foods during which the young woman is adorned with jewels, flowers, and the finest clothing.

Japan

In previous generations, a special dish of sweet mochi rice and red adzuki beans called sekihan was served to a girl when she had her first period. The dish was kept secret from the extended family until it was served, and then the reason for the special celebration was discretely understood without anyone saying anything. Sekihan is still served at special occasions such as birthdays, but the tradition of serving it to mark menarche is not as common.

Latin America

A *Quinceañera* is a familiar tradition in Latin American culture during which a girl is symbolically escorted into womanhood by her family when she turns fifteen. The roots are attributed to Aztec ceremonies, but now the grand fiesta usually begins with Mass and is followed with a large party. The young woman, adorned in a fancy dress, dances with her father, then her mother usually takes her to a "throne" where a tiara is placed on her head. Her father removes her sandals and slips on her first pair of high heels before leading her back to the dance floor. No longer a child, she is now viewed in her community as a woman.

Philippines

Many families continue to honor a daughter's eighteenth birthday with a traditional Debut, which is a celebration of life and what is to come. The ceremony is a formal affair and can become as extravagant as a wedding. It often includes a family procession, a prayer or blessing, and traditional dress. The young woman is honored with eighteen Treasures, which are meaningful gifts given by eighteen friends who were carefully selected as her event entourage. The gifts demonstrate how well each of the friends know the debutante.

A meaningful father-daughter dance is followed by a birthday cake and a speech by the young woman during which she can express her thoughts on life and her gratitude to her parents, extended family, and friends.

Europe

Debutante (French for "female beginner") describes young women of high society throughout Europe and the United Kingdom. Movies have given us many historical images of how young women from aristocratic backgrounds were introduced into society at formal events once they reached maturity. These matchmaking occasions allowed young women who were old enough to marry to be presented to eligible bachelors within an approved circle.

For several centuries debutantes in upper circles of British society were prepared for the Social Season when they would be presented at court in hopes of being noticed by a suitable bachelor. Queen Elizabeth II abolished the ceremony in 1958. After that, the tradition became increasingly insignificant due to the withdrawal of the royal influence.

However, in Austria the social season continues to thrive from January through March, when twenty-five formal balls are held in Vienna. Carefully selected debutantes glide across the dance floor with enough elegance to keep young girls dreaming of coming of age with visions of castles and princes.

Africa

In urban Kenya, ancient traditions are changing as this current generation of leaders has implemented various Alternative Rites of Passage Programs. Many are conducted through churches and have had a positive effect on the preteen boys and girls who go through the yearlong sessions separately. Often the training culminates with an exciting adventure-ceremony, such as climbing Mount Kenya to both test and celebrate their transition into adulthood.

Girls are awarded documents at the end of the ceremony that serve as tangible evidence of their transition from girls to young women. This is vastly different from the diminishing tradition of female circumcision that has long been common in parts of Africa as well as in the Middle East.

Canada

The Nootka tribe on the west coast of Canada is known for placing a high value on a young woman's physical endurance because it proves that she is ready to face the rigors of motherhood. The rite of passage for girls at the time of their menarche is to be rowed out into the Pacific Ocean where they are left in the frigid water and expected to swim to shore. The village watches and waits to either greet her or to send a rescue party.

When we enlarge our view of the world we deepen our understanding of our own lives.
Yo-Yo Ma

The Global Commonality

One mom who wrote to me said that her daughter wanted to know about all the options of what she could use when she started her period. The two of them always enjoyed online shopping together so it was natural for them to spend an evening side by side, scrolling.

The mom found it easy to explain why various sizes and thicknesses of pads are available as well as how an applicator works. The search brought up an array of related products, so the conversation included discussion of body odors and the best way to dispose of used items.

They chose all the essentials during their online shopping spree and added a few other recommended products. When the shipment arrived, the daughter eagerly awaited the first time she would need to use the pads, whether she started at home or school.

During their online search, they discovered that an estimated 500 million girls and women globally do not have adequate resources and knowledge to properly care for themselves during their periods.

A bit more research led the mother and daughter to websites that suggested ways they could serve as a team to provide education for women in a rural area outside their community. They helped to raise awareness about the lack of supplies and initiated a local donation drive.

If your daughter perks up at the idea of doing something like that, here are some topics for deeper discussion.

Staying Healthy

Many products are now created using natural fibers and without plastic. They have no potentially harmful chemicals such as bleach. Have you tried a variety of products? You might want to test out some new options yourself so that when your daughter is ready, you'll be able to recommend your favorites. This is an especially helpful idea if you've been using the same product for decades and have nothing to compare it with.

One mom told me she made her own washable pads

when she had health issues from the manufactured brands. Her daughter wanted her own custom fit pads and came up with a variation on her mom's design. The experience was an unexpected chance for more discussions and a woman-to-woman bonding time.

Include in your conversations with your daughter the topic of cramps. They shouldn't always be dismissed by a mom as simply part of every girl's monthly experience.

One young woman told me how she was diagnosed with a serious health issue; her mom had told her for eight years the pain was just normal cramps. The daughter had nothing to compare the pain to. Her mother thought she was being a baby even though the daughter was doubled over and felt like she was going to pass out. I'm sure the mother felt terrible when she discovered her daughter's level of pain was very real, as was her health issue.

If you have any question about your daughter's health, take her in for a consultation with your physician. Let your doctor eliminate all the options that can range from endometriosis and cysts to ovarian tumors and cervical cancer. Even if you daughter is told after a round of tests that what she's experiencing are, indeed, cramps, at least she will have a starting point to know what's normal and how to manage the pain.

Help her to learn how to express where it hurts and identify the level of the pain. Ask your doctor about all the options for treatment rather than accepting the standard directive to "take two and call me in the morning." By being your daughter's advocate, you're helping her to learn how to express what she feels and showing her how to go about obtaining help when she needs it.

History of Feminine Products

Up until the last two hundred years, it is generally believed that menstruating women cared for their bodies by using absorbent aids found in nature such as moss, sea sponges, wool, parchment, or cloth. Not a lot of details are known. You can, however, find plenty of information on the products developed in modern times and the marketing that propelled them into use. If your daughter is interested in knowing more, here's a brief summary for you to share.

1860s

Nurses, including some who served during the Civil War, noticed that the wool pulp bandages used for severe wounds were extremely absorbent. They used the bandages during their cycles instead of the traditional layers of rags because the material was cheap and disposable.

1888

The first disposable pads entered the market. They were developed by Johnson & Johnson and advertised as Lister's Towels.

1890s

Catalogs discretely advertised "Absorbent Health Napkins" and "Ladies Faultless Serviette Supporters." These pads were made of sateen, which was soft but not particularly absorbent, and were held in place by a large rubber band around the hips. An elastic "Hoosier Sanitary Belt" was designed that allowed women to affix washable pads to the belt.

1910s

"Sanitary aprons" were offered in catalogs as "Bloomer Shields." They tied around the waist and provided a swath of waterproof material between the legs that was designed to protect clothing. Absorbent cloth was used to line the sling of the apron.

1921

Kimberly Clark developed Kotex pads from the same cellulose material that was originally used in the Lister's Towels. It was held in place with an elastic belt that had metal hooks in front and back.

1929

A male doctor developed the first tampon with his patented telescoping cardboard applicator. A woman bought his patent and began producing and marketed tampons through her female-led company.

1932

A group of midwives patented an early version of the first menstrual cup made of rubber. Other patented versions were developed over the decades, but they didn't become commercially viable until 2001 when the Mooncup was introduced.

1980s

Pads with adhesive strips that could attach to underwear were developed, and the sanitary belt soon went off the market. A commercial industry grew as a variety of shapes, sizes, and thickness of the pads were offered in stores.

2000s

The Mooncup or Menstrual cup became available on a broad scale and was made from high-grade silicone, which provided hypoallergenic properties as well as durability. Period Underpants gained popularity and were created in a variety of sizes with different features. Reusable tampons and pads also become an option as patterns and instructions became easily accessible online.

After collecting this information, I felt a greater empathy for what my grandmother and the women before her had to do each month in order to care for themselves hygienically. I also saw why so much secrecy and unspoken distain was attached to menstruation. Can you see it, too? This insight gave me even more reason to release all residual hurts from my childhood. The women in my family were among many who avoided any potentially uncomfortable conversations with their daughters.

Let's change the stigmas for our daughters and equip them to have healthy, reverent, and grateful views of their bodies. What a beautiful change it would be if young women paused to be grateful and whispered an honest prayer at their menarche by saying, "Thank You, God, for making me a woman and for blessing my body this way."

It begins with you, dear moms.

Stories from Other Moms and Daughters

When Grandma Arrived

I didn't begin to develop until I was thirteen. As soon as my mother noticed, she made me start wearing loose-fitting tops and told me that "Ama," my grandmother, was going to come from Taiwan for an important visit within the year. I had only seen my grandmother three times, so I was excited. I didn't realize that I was the reason for her long journey until I saw the wrapped gifts in her suitcase. She said all of them were for me, but I couldn't open them until we had our tea and *Yuebing* or Moon Cakes.

Moon Cakes are round pastries that have a thin crust and different kinds of fillings. Ama brought Moon Cakes with mung bean paste and some with green tea filling.

The next afternoon, when I came home from school, the dining room table was set with China plates and teacups. A plate of the promised Moon Cakes and a pot of expensive Oolong tea was in the center of the table, and all the gifts were waiting by my place. Ama was seated at the head of the table and had on a beautiful, red silk brocade top. She quoted a poem or something in Taiwanese, and we drank the tea and ate the Moon Cakes in silence. My mom and Ama kept smiling at me.

I was finally told I could open the presents, and they

explained that these were gifts for a woman, not a child. I unwrapped pretty things like simple pieces of jewelry, a scarf, and a fancy pen. Ama said the gifts were from the women relatives in my family, who had been given these gifts when they each left childhood.

That's when I began to understand what the ceremony was all about. I had picked up enough details about the facts of life over the years, and I was old enough to feel comfortable with all the unspoken elements of the gentle, solemn, and private ceremony. I liked feeling that I was now included with the women in my family. I told my Ama how honored I was that she had come all the way to our home at this time in my life.

I have no idea if what my mom and grandma did for me was specifically linked to our Taiwanese culture, or if it was something developed over the years between the women in my extended family. The tradition lives on, though, because I have a second cousin in Canada whose daughter will be twelve this year. She asked if I would be willing to share one of my "woman's gifts" for the upcoming tea party she was planning. I've saved all the presents I received and decided to send the porcelain butterfly pin. I think I'll include a note and tell her to spread her wings and fly into adulthood.

Oh, the Possibilities!

What are some ways that you might put the thoughts from this chapter into action? What portions of the chapter stood out to you?

Here's a list of possible points of action:

• Do some research on your family heritage and culture and talk with your daughter about those customs.

• Keep up a family tradition or start one between the women in your family.

• If your daughter adores history, let her research your family tree and invite her to share her findings in a way that feels most comfortable to her—at the family dinner table, alone with you, or in a written report that serves double duty as a homework assignment or extra credit.

• Try a recipe connected to your family heritage. Include your daughter in the preparation of the traditional food and add other cultural touches, such as learning a few words in the language that your great-grandparents spoke or music specific to their culture.

• Use the discussions of your heritage as a chance to instill respect for other cultures. Elevate her understanding of what it means to honor others while retaining your own foundational culture, traditions, and sacred beliefs.

NOTES

*Many women do noble things,
but you surpass them all.*

Proverbs 31:29, NIV

My Hope for You

I hope this book gives you freedom not to be chained to anything in your past. Shame off you, grace on you. I hope that you have drawn closer to God and felt a new sense of gratitude that He created you exactly the way He did and made you a beautiful woman.

I also hope this book enables you to do something— anything—that will show the daughter in your life that you esteem her, are there for her, and deeply love her.

I hope you pray for your daughter more than you ever have before. We can't fully grasp the power that prayer has in the unseen world. What we do know is that God has healed relationships in amazing ways, prodigal daughters have returned home, and women succeeded—through prayer—not to turn out to be "just like their mothers."

Keep praying. For yourself, for your daughter, and for the two of you together.

Another hope is that you will learn the fine art of dreaming alongside your daughter rather than dreaming for her. That way you'll be able to celebrate together when her dreams come true.

My final hope for you is that you'll understand at the heart-level who you are in Christ. As mentioned, the list "What God Says about You" has been included on the following pages. It can be a valuable resource for your daughter and you to use together as a study guide.

I've also included a piece from my journal that I wrote for my daughter as I watched her being an amazing mom to her children. It's entitled "More Than" and first appeared in print in a small gift book I wrote, *A Pocketful of Hope for Mothers*.

May there be many meaningful conversations between your daughter and you for years to come. And may the next generation and generations beyond reap the rich rewards of the intentional efforts you make to honor and celebrate your daughter when you welcome her into womanhood.

More Than

More Than
A Poem for My Daughter

I was wrong.
My darling daughter, I was wrong.
I told you that you were enough.
Enough woman, mother, chef, teacher, puppeteer. . .
Today I saw the deeper truth as I watched you accomplish
heroic acts of everyday motherhood.
Now I know that you are not enough.
No.
The truth is. . .
you are more than.
More than
the length of your days
or the breadth of your knowledge.
More than
yesterday's accomplishments
or tomorrow's goals.
You are more than you were when you started this journey into
motherhood.
More than
a diaper-changing station
or a twenty-four-hour concession stand.
You are more than you can see;
more than your thin emotions can feel.
You are more than the sum of all your parts.

More than what you saw in the mirror this morning.
More than what you told yourself three minutes ago.
Listen. Hear this and treasure it in your heart.
You don't have to
do more
be more
give more
try more.
You already are more.
More than you know.
You are
a song in the night
a gentle touch
a calm word
an assuring smile
a soft kiss.
You are not just enough, dear little mama.
You are more than.
In all things, for all days,
you are more than a conqueror through Him who
handcrafted you
unfailingly loves you
continually guides you.
He is the One who placed on you the care of these eternal
souls—
the Giver of all good gifts.
The One who is
and was
and is to come.
He will give you more than enough to see you through.

What God Says about You

What God Says about You

You were made in My image. (Genesis 1:27)

You are My treasured possession/peculiar treasure. (Exodus 19:5)

If you seek Me with your whole heart, you will find Me. (Deuteronomy 4:29)

Delight in Me and I will give you the desires of your heart. (Psalm 37:4)

When you are brokenhearted, I am close to you. (Psalm 34:18)

I know everything about you. (Psalm 139:1)

I know when you sit down and when you stand up. (Psalm 139:2)

I am familiar with all your ways. (Psalm 139:3)

I knit you together when you were in your mother's womb. (Psalm 139:13)

You are fearfully and wonderfully made. (Psalm 139:14)

All your days were written in My book before there was one of them. (Psalm 139:15-16)

My thoughts towards you are as countless as the sands on the seashore. (Psalm 139:17-18)

As a shepherd carries a lamb, I have carried you. (Isaiah 40:11)

I knew you before you were conceived. (Jeremiah 1:4-5)

My plans for your future are for good, to give you hope. (Jeremiah 29:11)

I have loved you with an everlasting love. (Jeremiah 31:3)

I will never stop being good to you. (Jeremiah 32:41)

I will take pleasure in doing good things for you and will do those things with all My heart and soul. (Jeremiah 32:41)

I want to show you great and marvelous things. (Jeremiah 33:3)

I rejoice over you with singing. (Zephaniah 3:17)

I am your provider. I will meet all your needs. (Matthew 6:31-33)

I know how to give good gifts to My children. (Matthew 7:11)

I gave you the right to become My child when you received My Son, Jesus, and believed in His name. (John 1:12)

I have been misrepresented to you by those who don't know Me. (John 6:41-44)

I have prepared a place for you. I will come back for you and take you to Myself so that we can be together forever. (John 14:3)

I love you even as I have loved My only Son. (John 17:23)

I revealed My love for you through Jesus. (John 17:26)

I determined the exact time of your birth and where you would live. (Acts 17:26)

In Me you live and move and have your being. (Acts 17:28)

I am for you and not against you. (Romans 8:31)

I will never allow anything to separate you from My love for you. (Romans 8:35-39)

I gave My Son so that you and I could be reconciled. (2 Corinthians 5:19)

I am your peace. (Ephesians 2:14)

I am able to do more than you could possibly imagine. (Ephesians 3:20)

I am at work in you, giving you the desire and the power to fulfill My good purpose for you. (Philippians 2:13)

I revealed the exact representation of Myself through Jesus. (Hebrews 1:3)

Every good gift you receive comes from Me. (James 1:17)

I did not give you a spirit of fear but of power, love, and self-control. (2 Timothy 1:7)

I desire to lavish My love upon you because you are My child and I am your Father. (I John 3:1)

I gave the ultimate expression of My love for you through Jesus. (I John 4:10)

My love for you is not based on your love for Me. (I John 4:10)

I am the complete expression of love. (I John 4:16)

I will dwell with you in heaven. You will be My people. I will be your God. (Revelations 21:3)

I will one day wipe away every tear from your eyes and there will be no more crying or pain or sorrow. (Revelation 21:4)

I have written your name in My book. (Revelation 21:27)

I invite you to come. (Revelation 22:17)

Christy Miller

The High School Years
Meet tender-hearted Christy Miller and her Forever Friends in this 4-book series

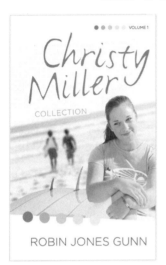

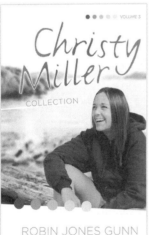

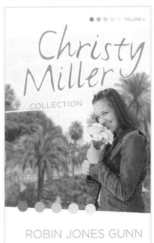

 ChristyMillerShop.com

Non-Fiction

Spoken For:
Embracing Who You Are and Whose You Are

ChristyMillerShop.com

Non-Fiction

Praying for Your Future Husband:
Preparing Your Heart for His

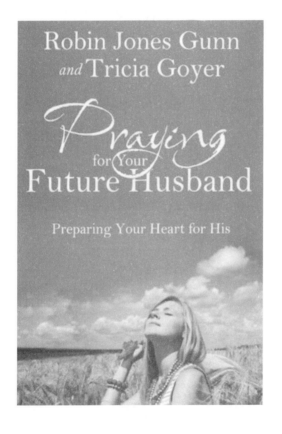

Non-Fiction

Victim of Grace
Robin's Poignant Memoir

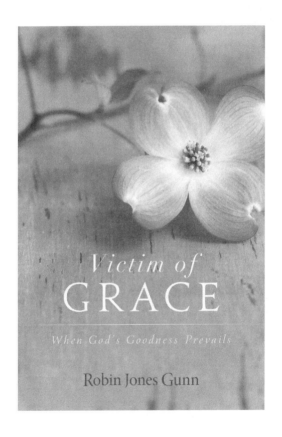

ChristyMillerShop.com

Bestselling Haven Makers Series

When Young Moms Gather, Friendships Grow

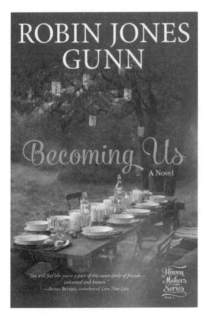

For a list of
all of Robin's books
and free downloads,
visit

 ChristyMillerShop.com
RobinGunn.com